Intelligence for Management

Attention Authors

Manas Publications is fighting a war to tell the world that India can win the battle not only by the bullet but also by pen. We are converting fighters into writers. There is no dearth of intellectuals in our country, however, their knowledge is confined to them only. No sincere effort has been made by any other publisher to channelise their knowledge, which is why the talent of every intellectual remains latent. An author always presents the raw material in the shape of a manuscript and it is the job of the publisher to convert it to a finished product. Manas has been continually motivating intellectuals and publishing their manuscripts for more than two decades and would like to publish your manuscript too. If you or your colleagues have a manuscript ready for publication or are working on it, contact us with a detailed synopsis and list of contents. Manas will also suggest you a suitable title for writing related to your area of expertise. Manas is known for its publishing quality. We take utmost care in publishing and also give wide publicity to the book and its author through our national and international distribution network.

Intelligence for Management

DC Pathak, IPS
Former Director, Intelligence Bureau, India

Manas Publications
New Delhi-110002 (INDIA)

MANAS PUBLICATIONS
(Publishers, Distributors, Importers & Exporters)
4402/5-A, Ansari Road
(Opp. HDFC Bank)
Darya Ganj, New Delhi-110 002 (INDIA)
Off. ✆ 23260783, 23265523, Res. ✆ 23842660
Fax: 011-23272766
E-mail: manaspublications@vsnl.com
www.manaspublications.in

ISBN 978-81-7049-377-8
Rs. 495

Typeset at
Manas Publications

Printed in India at
RK Offset Works, Delhi
and published by Mrs Suman Lata for
Manas Publications, 4402/5-A, Ansari Road
(Opp. HDFC Bank),
Darya Ganj, New Delhi-110 002 (INDIA)

Dedicated

to my grand-children – Adya, Ananya, Naman, Ishaan and Somya

Contents

Preface

Mind is the brain's software and intelligence is its programmer. We need knowledge updates to function intelligently. Intelligence is an instrument of rationality and a determinant of scientific outlook. It also equips a person with the sense of understanding of what confidentiality is which is a gift given by nature only to human beings. The application of intelligence in analysis, assessment and decision-making will always be a measure of an individual's personal achievement and an index of competitive advantage.

Human intelligence can achieve the capability of peeping into the future not through clairvoyance but through an analytical projection of knowledge into the area of anticipation. Having intelligence and being intelligent are not exactly the same thing for it is the exercise of intelligence through action towards one's own good that completes the process of being intelligent.

All business is human activity and a corporate body is also basically a conglomerate of people bonded by a sense of identification with the enterprise and a commitment to the firm's operational expanse. The fortune of a company is largely determined by the quality of its human resource.

The unprecedented transformation of the world in 1990s in terms of geo-politics, world economy and global security has hastened the process of globalization in which borderless markets, competitiveness and the advent of knowledge economy have become the prime movers of growth. The new found importance of information and its precious variant, the competitive intelligence, has overtaken the world of business and commerce as all strategic and operational decisions of an enterprise today have to be rooted in knowledge.

Both leaders and workers have to be adept at acquiring and evaluating information. Where knowledge is deep and application is intense there is prospect of innovation. The age of information has changed the concept of leadership itself inasmuch as it has replaced the notions of charisma with the new requirement of the leader having to take knowledge-based decisions. The challenge of human resource development lies in the new task of having to convert the work force, earlier looked upon as a manual congregation, into an assembly of knowledge workers each of whom is a contributor to the organisation's overall progress.

We are knocking at the doors of the 'age of intelligence' and this is already impacting on the accepted concepts of 'success', 'life-work balance', 'freedom of choice', 'social responsibility' and 'cross-culture mobility'. Since open information is shared universally no sooner than it is produced, the challenge is to churn it into intelligence whereby its owner may be in a position to visualize an opportunity or detect a danger signal, ahead of others. This infact has already set off an open-intelligence movement in which even for national security, collation and analysis of overt information has become as important as the access to covert sources of intelligence.

The new 'globalized' world is pressing for a paradigm shift in the methodology of management in all spheres—personal or business related. The need for equipping organizations with the tools to tackle the future is demanding a reinvention of management and a conscious discarding of structures and styles that suited the status-quo approach. It is remarkable how the working of a classical intelligence organization—whose agenda always is to look at what lies ahead, has many conceptual offerings to make to the modern management in this age of rapid change. Businesses confronting a volatile and unforgiving environment must drastically reduce the pull of the past, recognize that planning for too long a range is of limited value as new developments would force material changes, and think of structural reorganization that creates fluid project-based units. These three basics of management have been the hallmark of all intelligence organizations because of the very nature of their work. Being intelligent in business means being smart about understanding these organizational challenges of change.

This book is the last in the trilogy of my work on applied intelligence after the two published earlier- "Intelligence: A Security Weapon" and "Intelligence: Corporate Security and Vigilance". They define the relevance of this subject respectively for nations, organizations and individuals. Intelligence orientation is an essential component of the process of upgradation of the human resource in any organization that is on test for performance and productivity.

In these forty odd years of my association with the profession of intelligence I have seen the evolution of communication technology transforming the process of information—gathering and information handling. The switch from teleprinters to satellite phones enabled all organizations to become more flat and lean. Speed of the relay of the content became the defining requisite of decision-making in the 'age of information' that came about with the advent of IT revolution. In less than two decades, however, another paradigm shift is on the horizon by way of a transition to the 'age of intelligence'. The pace of communication is in a sense giving way to the primacy of the content again because what is needed for success is intelligence – not mere information. Intelligence is a kind of knowledge that has to be accessed through special efforts or uncovered with the help of analytical tools.

In this new transition it is the competitive intelligence that would determine the prospects of a firm acquiring and retaining an advantage. Successful executives and business leaders have to understand and absorb the conceptual meanings of the terms like 'information', 'knowledge', 'intelligence', 'intellectual property' and 'restrictive security'. The strategies of recruitment, evaluation and due diligence need to be reset and the business schools need to upgrade their management courses to meet the requirement of the new age.

The book is meant as much for corporate leaders and intelligence professionals as for the informed public at large.

DC Pathak, IPS

1 Being Well-Informed

Today ignorance is the bliss no more. In the age of information, being intelligent means being well-informed for this indeed is a pre-requisite for success. There are three crucial indicators on which such a person is tested. First of all, a well-informed individual has the right information for taking the right course of action, in time. Secondly, in terms of reliability and completeness, the information on which action is based should be of a class that makes a difference between a decision and a guess. And finally, in a fast moving world being well-informed cannot be a one time goal or achievement. A person has to remain continually well-informed. The personal or professional situation may change compelling a re-evaluation of the line pursued. Some new information may come in to warrant a change in the response option.

The dynamics of being well-informed include an awareness of one's own persona and identification of the drags and bounces in the competitive environ. To make use of it all you have to have a pro-active attitude, tempered by objectiveness and rationality. According to its simplest definition 'information' is a meaningful data or fact that tells you what you did not already know.

Information thus has the profound effect of 'grading' people into those who command knowledge that was specifically needed and those who do not have it. Being well-informed requires an understanding of your own potential in relation to the strong points and inadequacies of the person you are dealing with and a good knowledge of the various facets of the environ in which you are placed. If you are in business you have to have a comprehensive idea of the competition that exists around you and the factors that set the competitive environ. They include the politico-legal regime, the socio-cultural spread, the level of economic and technological development, the law and order situation and the potential of the market in your field of operation. A well-informed individual or corporate entity would have a lesser risk of running into unpleasant surprises. Innocence does not help and awareness of where you stand and what others are like, is crucial to your own well-being.

Being well-informed is intrinsic to being in a position to act and to lead. Today much of the charisma of a 'leader' is attributable to his or her ability to take quick knowledge-based decisions. This is what strengthens the view that leaders are not born but made. The leader has to be a well-informed person because for him, more than ever before, 'it is pardonable to be defeated but not to be surprised'.

We live in an age where huge amounts of information and communications are pouring in from outside. A large volume of ideas is generated within our own minds as well. We may get drowned in the mass of data or needlessly get stuck to our ideas out of a sense of attachment to them. We have to consciously scan them for their utility. We often see without observing, observe without absorbing and absorb without making a distinction between what is important and what is less significant. If we can eliminate this deficiency, we will find it a lot easier to fix our priorities. I remember one of my bosses who guided me through the initial years of my career in intelligence, repeatedly reminding me of two things. He would often say that 'routine is important' and also tell me that one should 'distinguish essentials from non-essentials'. I later realized that these two formulations corresponded to the two vitals of the tree of life–the base or the 'roots' that had to be regularly tended and the 'flowers' whose appearance alone signified the essence of growth–the ultimate 'essential' for the tree.

Today, it is the exchange of information that sets the pace for the free market enterprise. The speed of transmission of business intelligence determines the fortunes at the market place. The earlier you access information of intelligence value the quicker will be your response to the challenge of change. Well-informed people are able to generate new strategy options ahead of others. An intelligent organization makes sure that the pathways of information movement within the enterprise are clearly defined and continually used. In the 1980s the General Motors became the first low cost producer of automobiles after it acquired Electronic Data Systems (EDS) at a cost of $ 2.5 billion and switched over to fully automated production lines, securing an early-bird advantage. In recent years instant communication has revolutionized the distance learning programmes and globalized the campus network creating new businesses for the universities.

A well-informed person finds it easier to get to the heart of any matter. Such an individual has a fuller awareness of the cause and effect relationships that shape events and can understand the unintended consequences of one's action better. Moreover, such a person is resistant to the failings that arise from the so-called 'group think' syndrome. The Independent 9/11 Commission in the USA reprimanded the intelligence analysts there for succumbing to this malady in which the desire to reach unanimity overtakes the regard for facts. Being well-informed helps to preserve autonomous thinking against the tendency to fall in line with the views of the majority. It strengthens the freedom to stick to the truth amidst pressures from above or in the face of peer opposition. It saves the person from the consequences of jumping to conclusions on inadequate data. A well-informed person is not easily offended.

In the era of globalization a new advantage of being well-informed is that you enhance your ability to make a difference locally if you are knowledgeable in the global sense. This does not mean having a volume of information; it means having the knowledge that enables you to see what is immediate around you, in a wider perspective and locate the key point of it all. You are aware of the competitive environ around and have an idea of the potential players who could come on to your turf from distant locations. An intelligent organization continues to look at the alternatives to its current processes and product applications and is vigilant against the possibility of the competition springing upon it a surprise variant in its business area. A conscious effort to visualize what competition can possibly do, is an exercise that should be undertaken from time to time. A well-informed person is, however, not deterred by this thought as he is seized of the exciting prospect that the future, he believes, holds for him at any point of time.

An important dimension of being well-informed is to have a certain completeness of knowledge in the sense of having awareness also of those related matters or spheres that impact on the pursuit at hand. In the complex world of today knowledge comes in integral packages because of which everybody faces the growing challenge of having to keep abreast of all those matters that complement a given subject or area of knowledge. Today, a successful teacher should know that there are high levels of stress amongst the students. The owner of a BPO that runs night shifts must be aware of the issues of personal security of the girl employees as also of the laws relating to sexual harassment of women at the place of work. Knowledge is not meaningful unless it is integral in the sense that it adequately covers all relevant facets of the task that is being taken up.

That knowledge comes in integral packages is the concept that is ultimately helping out the world's IT infrastructure already under severe stress from the computing tasks and on way to becoming overwhelmed by the unprecedented data being generated today. A new model called 'cloud computing' is on the horizon in which processing, storage and networking will revolve around particular tasks.[1] A new level of system intelligence will be made available to facilitate the quest for information concerning diverse subjects and areas ranging from traffic management to retail.

It is in crisis management that the importance of being well-informed comes into play in a big way. A crisis seems daunting because you often do not have all the information you need for diagnosing what has gone wrong and where. If you can determine quickly as to how did the crisis originate you would be so much closer to the right response by way of taking the first steps towards damage control. You will be able to quarantine the affected part so that the rest of the enterprise and its operations maintained full functionality. Efficacy of the damage control effort would depend greatly on the soundness of the information base made available to the leadership.

A crisis is caused by an internal source or an external factor, very often the former. It may be relatable to the doing of a malcontent within the enterprise, failure of some process, an assault from an adversary outside, an unanticipated change in the competitive environ or a sheer accident. Although each crisis is different from the other, there is merit in the company keeping contingency plans ready for all foreseeable disruptions. In the ultimate analysis the smart thing is to avert a crisis by laying down an intelligence-based monitoring system that would give out warning signals of an impending breakdown or irregularity. Intelligence alone can preempt a mishap that is not purely accidental. Man-made disasters can be checked if the organizations take to good internal processes such as rigorous hiring methods, strict performance reviews and intensive training programmes designed to protect the personnel from internal and external debilitation and threats.

Experience in the corporate world has shown that a big business crisis is often preceded by undetected indicators of an insider committing an irregularity or a product or process having a problematic run over a period of time. In many cases internal vigilance failed to step in to prevent the outbreak because the alarm signals were either overlooked or underestimated. A leadership, if it claims to be well-informed, should not be oblivious of the rumours and whispers circulating within the organization and should know when to take cognizance of the same.

Information savvy people have better prospects of remaining well-informed. Such people have certain traits and habits that can be emulated by others. An information conscious person reads a lot and has a way of categorizing and docketing information that he has come across. He tends to prefer authentic opinions and disregards gossip. He has a healthy interest in human psychology and behaviour that enables him to handle interactions with others competently and get the best out of them in terms of gaining knowledge. An information savvy person has the discipline of a logical bend of mind, which guides him in his quest for knowledge. He does not run into 'information overload' because he does not clog his mind with non-essential data.

Being intelligent means being able to put information to its best use for one's own self. If you do not think you have enough facts to make an informed decision, do your homework until you are confident about your decision. Remember, in the age of information organizational learning is what raw material was in the industrial age. Intelligent people therefore make sure that they have the benefit of a free, frank and critical interaction within their organization that leads to knowledge creation and contributes to their decision-making.

While there is a compelling need for widening the orbit of access to information, well-informed persons make full use of the skills of observation to open the doors of knowledge. They can get a lot out of merely watching an individual's conduct. They have a knack of deciphering the social trends and organizational behaviour from manifestations that the others would find unintelligible. They are aware that in the complex cause and effect relationships of our times, many developments have to be viewed together to read the new social values or structures that were shaping up. They can visualize how several new phenomena may have been triggered off by one incident or social experience.

The geo-political impact of the disintegration of the USSR and the rise of a new global security scenario in the wake of 9/11 are illustrative of the challenges that only information savvy people would be able to handle by way of making the right readings about the consequences of such events. Not everybody would be able to understand that 9/11 had the effect of undermining the mathematical model of forecasting and establishing the primacy of 'alternate case scenarios' as the basis of assessments. It also brought home the awareness of the new kind of sabotage–the destruction of information base of an enterprise in a terrorist attack. Further, 9/11 changed the concept of war and introduced the new format of the 'asymmetric warfare'. It brought to the fore the importance of fool-proof methods of identification and authentication, gave a big boost to biometrics and created a new security imperative of preserving backup data in diverse locations.

There have been innumerable cases of businessmen going down because they stuck to the old ways and could not bring themselves to change. They were either not well-informed in terms of being aware of the fact that in the age of information, technological advancements would often prove transformative in their impact on business or were simply lacking in the ability to lead change. The leadership of an enterprise today is tested for its capacity to survive an innovative competitor who arrives on the scene with a product that holds better promise and is cheaper at the same time. If there is timely analysis of information to signal the emergence of a competition of this nature, a strategy of defence can be put into action.

If you are able to define the question about what you want to know, you can proceed to identify the potential source from where you can get it. The Government is a big holder of information, a significant part of which may not be in the public domain. Publications and internet are a major source of open information. There are companies and investigative agencies, which can garner information particularly needed by you, for a fee. If the information of your interest is in the possession of individuals or organizations that are in the rival camp, you may have to invoke skills used by intelligence professionals to get to that information covertly. You cannot, however, violate legal and ethical code in the process. You cannot steal trade secrets. You cannot plant bugging devices and you cannot intrude into somebody's privacy. In most situations information of intelligence value can be churned out of facts available in the open, through competent analysis and then utilized for decision-making.

A well-informed person keeps track of the new trends affecting the socio-economic scene around. The knowledge society is predictably seeing the rise of skill-based employment. The service sector is booming and is perhaps the largest employer of skilled hands. Services are based on special knowledge and skills. Indian education system kept churning out graduates who remained unemployed at a time when we had an unprecedented growth of a job market that was crying for skilled hands. Our systems need to get oriented to removing skills shortages as otherwise it will become very difficult to handle the brewing unemployment crisis. Those with a minimal formal education should have the opportunity of getting trained as nurses, mid-wives, paramedics, plumbers, telecom repairers, couriers, co-operative's managers, old home caretakers, retail storekeepers and crèche assistants. An intelligent entrepreneur can work on this scenario to create his own business.

It is difficult to imagine a leader who is not well-informed about the set up he is heading. If it is a business enterprise he has to be in the complete know of the merits and demerits of the performance of all members of his organization so that he can run a convincing system of rewards and recognition. A successful leader is accessible to his people and is in a position to give a definite guideline or response whenever some knotty issue pertaining to the internal working or the external environ travels up to him. A leader is where the buck stops. The imperative of being well-informed comes into play when a leader is called upon to creatively manage the enterprise down the line, in a manner that would enable it to work successfully in a scenario of change.

Endnote

1. *Harvard Business Review,* October 2009

2 You have to find Information; Information does not find you

Being intelligent means being observant and being observant means taking notice of whatever is significant in the scene around. The ability to discriminate between the important and the inconsequential in any situation is partly a gift of the nature but it is also something that can be acquired through application. It is the willingness to imbibe knowledge that defines the essence of being intelligent. In the process of observing and absorbing whatever is there in the present, an intelligent person can make meaningful interpretations of matters that lay unexplained in the past and perceive things that might belong to the domain of the future. The insightful deductions that Sherlock Homes makes out of the visuals infront of him look extra-ordinary but they are achievable.

Observing and absorbing come from consciousness and consciousness powers intelligence. Being intelligent is linked to a developed consciousness that helps you to scan your own moods and identify your own anxieties and anger. It enables you to maintain the right emotional content in your responses. This minimizes the wasteful dissipation of energy. Intelligence and a spiritual outlook have a certain natural convergence. Understanding this is the crux of being intelligent. You can be at ease with the uncertainties of the world when you are certain that you are taking an objective view of things and that you are in a state of freedom to do that. Clarity of vision and a dispassionate assessment of what you encounter, are the hallmarks of being intelligent.

Observing what is happening in the external world becomes more meaningful when it is accompanied by an effort to keep it untainted by your own personal prejudices and attachments. Ignorance of one's own attitudinal weaknesses or succumbing to them knowingly detracts from being intelligent. It makes you accept a distortion and affects your judgment, none of which can do any good. An intelligent person is a developed individual who imbibes information with discretion and acts on it with determination. The need to know and know quickly is the key factor dominating our business and personal lives, today.

While the skill of observation no doubt opens up the doors of knowledge, the globalized world is generating a compelling need for widening the orbit of access to information. Globalization is adding to the ever-increasing speed with which business is conducted, expanding the area of watch on the competitors and demanding a monitoring of the competitive conditions across the board. There is a constant pressure for more information and a quicker decision-making. Being intelligent means being able to do better with information that falls short of giving the complete picture. It means being able to reconstruct the picture with the minimum number of jig-saw pieces and generally to manage the chaos better. Being intelligent is all about enhancing your ability to use your observation power to perceive an opportunity or a threat ahead of others and respond to it to your advantage.

Observation holds the key to learning from others and also to self-knowledge. It reinforces the ability to absorb change, which is so vital for moving ahead in these times. The challenge of change is the biggest problem that both leaders and workers face today. New options have to be formulated and readiness has to be there for embracing experimentation to handle change. There is a lot of learning to be done by observing the experience of others in similar situations and analyzing the case studies on projects carried out elsewhere.

The basic skills of gathering information or intelligence are rooted in observation, absorption and a healthy curiosity about knowing more. Vast amount of published material and on-line data may have to be scanned. The cyber world is the biggest source of information. The impact of internet and the information revolution anchored by it, is seen in the near extinction that *Encyclopedia Britannica*, the iconic patriarch of all libraries and the ultimate summary of human knowledge, is facing[1].

Accessing human resources is more challenging. You have to identify them, find a way of approaching them and use your ability to cultivate them in order to have a meaningful interaction with them. Garnering information through clever questioning, reading the body language of the person and ascertaining what might have been left unsaid by him in a conversation – are all skills that are associated with intelligent interviewing. Being intelligent is certainly relatable to the success with which human interactions are conducted in pursuit of an information quest. The use of covert methods of collecting information such as a secret watch through human surveillance or clandestine video-monitoring and planting of bugging devices, are available only to those who are authorized by the State to do this for the cause of national security. The acquisition of information otherwise has to conform to the universally recognized legal and ethical parameters. These forbid stealing a trade secret or an employee, resorting to impersonation in an interaction and planting an eve's dropping device.

Information savvy people are adept at tapping information from both open sources as well as the channels that are subterranean. An overt source of information that is a product of the new knowledge era is the social networking site that is fast dominating the internet communication scene. The corporate world is beginning to accept this social medium as a vital tool of office communication. An important upshot of this is the facility it provides for communicating with people you have never met, befriending them and garnering information of your interest from them. Tata Consultancy Services (TCS) was said to be trying to leverage online social networking for knowledge creation in its organisation of 110,000 employees[2]. One can generate responses to an idea or theme and add to one's wisdom.

Being intelligent goes with the awareness that you have to find information; information does not find you. All cultural traditions recommend a pro-active approach to seeking knowledge. It helps the quest for information if you raise the right questions as to what you are looking for and why. You can then proceed to rationally identify the possible sources that need to be accessed. The information may be in the public domain in some publication or on the internet and may lead you to some specialized library. It may on the other hand be in the possession of some individuals who may or may not be easily reachable. A plan of approach may have to be formulated and pursued to get to such an individual. If there are reasons for the person not wanting to part with the information you need, the skills of the type that intelligence professionals use may have to be thought of, without of course violating the legal parameters. Intelligent people make the most of face-to-face sessions with their mentors and avail of skill exchanges with colleagues to build their knowledge. They also try to put their dormant skills to use for learning on the job.

These days there are commercial sources, which can give you the desired information for a fee. There are various kinds of investigative agencies who can dig out information for you from particular sources for a consideration. In a competitive environ the information you seek may be in the possession of individuals in the rival camp who would not furnish it to you unless you have won them over to an extent that for them retaining your friendship becomes more important than the risk they might run in the process of sharing the knowledge with you. Often it is easier to work through intermediaries and common contacts. Finally, in a situation where new frontiers of knowledge are opening up, the information you need may be unraveled only through a regular research. In anticipation of success, entrepreneurs are sponsoring and investing huge funds in stem-cell research, exploration of nanotechnology and discovery of sub-lethal weapons. In the information age quest for new knowledge is also good business.

Nobody knows everything: everybody knows something. This is what has made the new world turn to Wikipedia—the inter-active online encyclopedia written by every one. It is becoming the ultimate instant resource for information though the credibility factor has to be handled by the individual user accessing that information. The open source movement has established over the last decade or so in particular, a new collaborative approach facilitated by the inter-net for developing high quality information products. This is carrying forward the process of academic peer review established a log time ago that was based on the concept that knowledge could be evolved through consensus building.

A product of IT revolution is the emergence of an electronic network called Access Intelligent (AI) which connects hundreds of people in the defence, intelligence, law-enforcement, commercial and academic worlds. The network includes publicly available reports and personal observations. The importance of being able to connect, has produced new businesses. A company called Capital IQ aggregates marked data and information on executives to make it easy for anybody to find out who one could approach. Friendster also is of help in exploring connections inside and outside of companies around the world. Information of intelligence value coming from open sources is becoming increasingly important because of this new connectivity. Sources connected with the AI were able to report situations on the ground in Afghanistan to the crew of the American ships launching Afghan operations. Open source intelligence is becoming as valuable as anything received through a classified package. Being intelligent means being good at tapping the sources of information wherever they might be.

Observation and absorption, so necessary for information gathering, require concentration of mind. The mobile and high-tech age may be making people adept at 'multi-tasking' but one of its greatest casualties is our ability to focus on the matter at hand. For instance, to be in the present and be attentive to the colleague or client whom we have engaged in a conversation in the course of our own work, is not as easy as it sounds. We like to respond to e-mail messages during meetings or while on phone. In the process we are talking to someone but thinking about something else. Allowing minds to drift can lead to loss of information and the loss of an opportunity to meaningfully connect with others. Managing distraction is becoming a specialization on which a new kind of business of coaching is being created. A San Francisco based firm Mariposa Leadership and Illinois-based company called 'Dare to engage', work on the idea that attention can be bolstered through training[3].

In today's world everybody has to be attuned to handling information and responding to whatever seems to be answering the description of actionable intelligence. Adequate sharing of information in real time has acquired a new found importance. In fact collective intelligence that comes often from tapping the combined brain-power of large groups of people is becoming a new resource, which can lead to the collective good. From the hard area of national security to corporate well-being, information of intelligence value gleaned from the observations of the people at the grass roots can turn out to be of immense importance. 'Intelligence from below' is becoming a new instrument of national security in insurgency-affected territories and the areas impacted by organized crime. Encouraging citizens to take note of and input information on internet to the concerned decision-makers, has already created a major platform for ground level watch in developed societies.

Before you proceed to access any source of information outside of your organization you must checkout on whatever is available within your own enterprise. This is often not done. Each member of your workforce may have something to tell you about what is happening in the market and what the competition might be up to. He has come across things during his sales outings, business tours and even social interactions that could have a bearing on your organisation's plans. This tacit knowledge should not remain untapped. The organization's collective intelligence is called the 'wisdom of the crowd' and its importance as a knowledge resource is now being realized by all intelligent players in business. The cause of business intelligence is greatly helped if the organization uses cognitive diversity as a tool by permitting enough independence to its own people to see the content through different lenses. A healthy decentralization should mark the process of content management.

Paucity of information savvy managers is limiting the growth of knowledge economy. Experience of life that comes from observing human behaviour is an individual's exclusive asset. Being intelligent means being able to make this experience richer by sharpening the power of observation and handling all human interactions with a sense of interest and focus. Business schools would do well to upgrade their course content by highlighting the importance of information, intelligence gathering and knowledge generation. It is possible to learn the skills of accessing and handling information and using analysis as a tool for generating intelligence. In today's world these skills are an aid to success for all managers and business leaders who are required to take knowledge-based decisions.

In a globalized world someone who is an outgoing person is likely to be more successful. In fact being a bit of an extrovert pays and being an introvert certainly puts you on a discount. The requirement of the time is to be able to move across divisions or even around the world and to be able to communicate powerfully to motivate your people wherever they are – especially during tough times. Extroverts tend to forge relations with greater ease and have the additional advantage of being able to avail of opportunities of showing up to their seniors. If you are an introvert you should be the brain that runs the organization while the others are running the operations.

The search for information should be done with the belief that what you are looking for is there somewhere. This is what drives the researchers to explore all that is still in the realm of the future and try to unravel what is hitherto unknown. Entrepreneurs who by their imagination conclude that a new quest will bring success, become the sponsors of research. Such sponsors today are funding research as an investment in the business of knowledge creation that has an assured commercial use.

Framing and raising the right questions is the key to the unlocking of the fountain source of knowledge. Well-informed people know the importance of what, why and where, whenever they are looking for something. Intelligence professionals are particularly trained to work out the 'how' of the challenge of tapping an identified source of information. The skills they employ for garnering information from a human source, that might be a complete stranger or who for some reason might not be willing to share his knowledge with others, can be learnt and practised by anybody within the ambit of legal and moral constraints. All that this requires is an understanding of human psyche, an idea of the circumstances that exist around the particular person who is to be approached and a certain amount of confidence on the part of information seeker. As all intelligence is information about human activity, you get the best information from human sources.

Knowledge is the new driver of business along with land, labour and capital. In an explosion of unselected information the edge belongs to those who have the right information in time to make the best use of it. Timely information is crucial for managing change. The intelligence of a corporation does not come from the President or the top management; it comes mostly from the collective knowledge of all its members. People know more than they can tell or explain. Tacit knowledge is often of the class of intelligence and it lies with individual employees. It is not yet in the public domain because it has not been communicated to anyone. Drawn from experience it can provide the basis for making deductions for the future and trying out an innovation. Every product has a knowledge component that can be exploited to modify the offering for various sections of consumers. The organization must have a system of integrating the knowledge of all its segments. All R&D is an exercise in knowledge creation – the simplest version of it is the 'finding' that the workforce at the floor level of a plant may uncover to assist forward thinking of the organisation. Know-how is a combination of 'what and why' of a process and the tacit knowledge within an organization essentially revolves around it. Knowledge is a strategic resource and cost-effective knowledge management, therefore, is a big tool for achieving competitive advantage.

Inadequacy of information gathering and not the dearth of available information is often the reason why a business enterprise fails to take the right decisions. That is why most large players in business have a centrally controlled information center supervised by a top functionary. The group has people skilled in the business of accessing and analyzing information relevant to the enterprise. In today's world the leaders of trade and industry have to be information savvy, not feeling frightened of facing too much information and being prepared to absorb a brief. In the age of information all successful organizations have to have the ability to ensure that they do not suffer from knowledge deficit and do not end up acting on wrong information.

Endnotes

1. *Hindustan Times,* April 17, 2008 '*No takers for encyclopedia*',
2. *Hindustan Times,* March 9, 2008.
3. *Hindustan Times,* Career Gallery, September 16, 2008.

3 Intelligence is all about Human Activity

Intelligence basically plays on the human turf. It does not seek to predict acts of nature such as an earthquake or a process governed by the law of evolution. It is all about knowing what human beings are planning to do and how they might respond in a given situation. The study of human nature is the most fascinating of all the fields of knowledge. It not only gives us power in relation to others but also a control on our own working and choice. Societies rightly prescribed 'know thy self' as the first query in the pursuit of knowledge. Being intelligent involves so much of being good at handling inter-personal relations that in more cases than could be imagined, a project failure is the result not of lack of application of knowledge but of an inability to bring others on board. Behavioural scientists have written volumes, not in vain, on the importance of human interactions and chronicled lengthy self-improvement guides on how to make friends and win people.

Three decisive determinants of whether you have been intelligent in this sphere or not can be listed. The first has something to do with the widespread malady of one being too full of oneself while interacting with others. Sometimes this affliction is so pronounced that one does not let the other person have his or her say at all. An intelligent person listens to the other participant in an interaction and whenever necessary intervenes not to shut out the latter but to get a clearer idea of what that person was trying to say. This is getting the best results of your investment in time and energy over others. Most people can be flawed on this score. People deny themselves the benefit of learning from others just because they cannot help being short on listening and long on voicing their own views.

The second yardstick on which your intelligence is tested also relates to the fact that within your home and also from the moment you step out of your house, your life is anchored on interaction with other human beings – barring the time you might have kept entirely to your self for purposes like meditation or reading. Have you considered how many times during the course of inter-personal interactions you have stuck to first impressions and rushed to evaluate people without comprehensively knowing about them. Being too judgemental is a trait that intelligent people try to shed. This is at par with being hasty or thoughtless in action. It is possible that you have misinterpreted a situation because of your own hidden complexes and not because the other person had done something wrong.

It is better to try to judge a person from his actions rather than words because it is the former that signal his intention. Also, if you are able to read what the other person has left unsaid and interpret his body language, that would help. Judging a person is like taking a decision about him and an intelligent person always bases his decision-making on a competent analysis of the fuller data available on that subject. A related malady widely prevalent in our society is that people are too free with their criticism of others. This is a major spoiler of inter-personal relations. Criticism involves pointing out a flaw and not merely expressing a different opinion and therefore needs to be voiced with care. Sometimes a boss thinks he has the authority not only to criticize but also to tick-off a junior for something that had not turned out to be to the former's liking. It is necessary to remember that valid criticism should target a view or a stand taken by somebody and not the persona of the individual concerned. Often criticism is made in an idiom of bitterness because it originates from reactiveness. If you learn to respond rather than to react to whatever requires your comment, your critique will look more like a justifiable expression of disagreement for reasons that would have been made intelligible. You should be firm not foul in your language when criticizing anything.

The third crucial determinant of your success in inter-personal relations is your ability and willingness to convey your thanks and gratitude to the individual who has been helpful to you and has consciously done a good turn to you. If you do this you are not only being correct in the moral sense but also being intelligent. You have opened the way for a further advantage from him by inducing in him the desire to help you as an ally. The area of support and goodwill is never too big and an expression of gratitude is a fail-safe technique of enlarging this territory.

Not being a good listener, being too judgemental and being reluctant about saying 'thank you' is a deadly set of traits guaranteed to deny you the benefits of human interaction in both your personal and professional spheres.

It is intelligent not to let this mix of disabling attitudes grow on you. Higher the responsibilities you have on your shoulders the healthier you have to be in this area of the code of conduct.

Globalization has intensified movement of man and material across national and geographical boundaries. No place on earth today is too remote to be written off for human access. The world is now compelled to reckon with the concept first defined in the Indian Vedic thought that regarded the entire universe as one family - *Vasudhaiv Kutumbakam*. This is a call for embracing human beings wherever they may be and is particularly relevant as a management tip to the entrepreneurs, who wanted to extend their business to new areas. The ability to have an easy interaction with people of diverse ethnicities, cultures, languages, social values and traditions is a prerequisite for advancement of trade and commerce. Today only those business leaders and managers would be successful who can deal with the partners and customers across the global turf. Being intelligent means being open-minded and open-armed about such a calling and not letting your beliefs limit your vision of the shared values of life. Intelligent people do not allow cross-culture hurdles to obstruct their temporal and spiritual progress.

In the practical realm an intelligent enterprise understands that in global markets excellence of delivery cannot be achieved without an orientation towards the customer's socio-cultural responses in the country or the region of its location. All people function under the condition that their values, customs and biases impart to them and not necessarily out of rationality. Being intelligent means being able to analyze the customer's view of the product and to coin the promotional message in the light of this construct. It would be natural for a smart firm to give its country managers a long tenure in an area and a fair degree of delegation of the power of decision- making on behalf of the corporation. Such a corporation gains structural resilience by bringing in the country managers to perform at the corporate headquarters intermittently. In the process it tends to be flat which is a smart thing to do.

The most important part of the personality trait of a leader is his or her interpersonal competence. Leadership does not exist in a vacuum - a leader has to take others along. He cannot be the first among equals or an acknowledged guide unless he commands the image of being totally trustworthy in the eyes of those who look up to him. This image is achieved not through 'skill' development but is a product of commitment to values that is reflected in the leader's interaction with his followers. An intelligent person is able to impart the flavour of leadership to the handling of any work that involves others. Even when he is just carrying out an act of compliance he does this with distinction. He makes value addition through his intervention. This happens because being intelligent carries with it the promise of being a potential leader too.

There is a symbiotic relationship between leaders and followers - the leader supports and gives the follower a sense of growth and advancement and the follower makes his best effort in pursuit of the goal or the organization's mandate set by the leader. Many enterprises are over-managed and under-led. Successful leadership is inherently transformative in its impact because it achieves an excellent combination of idea and action in pursuit of the goal on one hand and of change and improvement, on the other. The leader uses the skills of handling human relations to the organization's best advantage. Effective companies build leadership in their managers as they move up. The brisk pace of business demands that a manager is able to take informed decisions without always looking over his shoulders. He may also have to implement a decision using whatever human resources were made available to him. Any such situation will test him for his leadership.

It is now widely recognized that human relations are best handled with an awareness of how emotions can shape the conduct and responses of any person. Both thinking and feeling, determine a person's reactions. Behavioural scientists use the term 'emotional intelligence' to describe the ability to understand emotions and manage them. It is not the triumph of heart overhead or the opposite of it but a unique intersection of both that helps to create optimal results in your understanding of your own self and of your relationship with others. If you integrate thinking and feeling you will live more effectively and be closer to rational decision-making. You can, during an interaction, scan your own feelings and also analyse the matrix of emotions in which the other person is placed. This will ensure that you remain objective, patient and accommodative both in personal situations as well as at the place of work. Intelligent people are emotionally competent. This is how they strengthen communication, improve inter-personal relationships and build successful teams. Someone has rightly said: 'CEOs are hired for their intelligence and business expertise, and fired for a lack of emotional intelligence.'

Understanding and handling human relations is necessary for brining a product closer to the users and for building a people-friendly image of a business enterprise. The corporate world is already looking upon the instrumentality of what is called the 'social compact' where people's forums are used to establish a grid between the manufacturers and the customers. An invisible advantage is accruing to those corporates that strike the right human relations while pursuing their business operations. The gap between the product and the customers is bridged if the management of the firm releasing the product promises affordable after-sales services as a part of this 'social compact'. The service sector is in fact becoming a part of this compact. The day is not far off when NGOs would get on to this 'social compact' territory for the general good. A new growth area is on the horizon where the corporate bodies can team up with NGOs for their mutual benefit and achieve synchronization between a cause and the commercial offering. All these initiatives reflect an entire range of new thinking and are anchored on the importance of successful human interaction for business.

Ideas and action constitute the run up to success. Both need human instrumentality. Setting a goal and striving to reach it comes only to human beings. The sense of achievement and a feeling of victory in a good cause is typically a human endowment. The essence of the mandate everybody is born with is to make a success of his or her life, to reach the goals envisaged and to use both intelligence and energy in that quest. Being intelligent means identifying the right fit of goals, concentrating on implementation and feeling the joy of active pursuit. You are focused on your progress and not distracted by needless comparisons with whatever is happening to others. The feeling of well being comes to you from your reaching the goal you had set for yourself and not from somebody else's failure to achieve his target.

Nobody's journey of life is complete unless it touches the lives of others. You would relish your achievement more if you had the satisfaction of having handled those human interactions well. The more you stir out and meet people and the more accessible you are to others, the greater would be the flow of information that helps your decision making.

The ability to handle people and get the best out of them can be developed through a conscious effort to understand human psyche, interact with others without ego or prejudices and recognize the play of cultural diversity. There are no fixed recipes on how to manage people. A business organization today can make progress only if it is successful in drawing upon the most valuable of its resources - the people. Growth is facilitated where relationships set the right internal and external environment for the enterprise and, in turn, bring synergy to the work force. The corporates are beginning to realize, belatedly, that in the equation - 'profit = sales - total expenses', there are hidden elements of loyalty, self esteem and the sense of organizational security that can enhance sales or output with only a little expenditure. It is the cost of failure on these invisible aspects of HRD that should drive the corporations to make this investment on their people.

Firms are human entities and when two of them enter into a joint venture, there has to be a meeting of hearts and minds between them so that a common clearing-house for important decisions can be established. A viable business alliance is much like two individuals joining hands in a partnership. Business partnerships often fail not because of reasons of profit and loss or the collapse of a strategy but due to failures of relationships.

It is an index of the importance of interpersonal relationships in any business enterprise that today companies are relying on human resource consultancy firms not only to handle recruitment and performance reviews for them but also to help them in the sensitive matter of firing any employees. The consultants meet the erstwhile employees, explain to them the facts and circumstances of the termination and do the necessary documentation of information for both sides. Outsourcing of HRD work is a fast growing industry not only because it could turn out to be cost-effective but also because the work requires special knowledge of human psyche and human relationships.

In real life the ability to build bridges between polarized people and ideas by making a creative use of diversity is in fact at the core of successful human resource management. Being intelligent means having an idea of the multiplicity of participants and factors at work in any situation and remaining open to connections that we could have missed. Intelligence lies in being aware that a relationship can enhance or degrade those involved in it. While our responses will be honed by our awareness of the limitations and certainties that exist in us they would also be influenced by our habits that got the better of our rationality. An intelligent person uses collaboration to generate energy and dialogue to generate wisdom. Intelligent people know that an attitude of openness to all ideas and patience to listen to others go a long way in giving them the best value out of any interactions. Sometimes it is possible to turn the stumbling block into a stepping-stone.

Globalization has intensified the competition for people and compelled the corporate world to look at the work force as an assembly of talented individuals. In human resource development emphasis is shifting from a mere recruitment of the right fit to the larger responsibility of fostering and retaining talent. There is a new found importance of getting the best out of each employee and putting a process in place that enables him or her to have a sense of participation in the overall growth. The strategy of handling business operations now covers the strategy of making the right invest on the human resource as well. This has given the human resource professionals a new leadership role in which they buildup the workforce that is available to the organisation. The hire and fire tradition, the boss-subordinate equations and the concept of reward and compensation have all changed in a globalized competition. All businesses are now people-centric and their success is determined largely by the loyalty and commitment of the men and women working for them.

Success today greatly depends on the use of the power of relationship not merely in the sense of networking as it is normally understood but more in terms of your keeping up the links with people even if they do not fulfill an immediate need. The immortal couplet of the famous Indian poet, Rahim, summarizes the wisdom of it all - 'when you get to befriend the high and the powerful do not drop your lesser acquaintances: remember where a needle is required to be used, a sword would not be effective'. The currency of real networking is not greed but generosity. Keith Ferrazzi[1] describes connecting as a constant process of giving and receiving help. You should become as willing to ask for help, as you are to give it. Intelligent people stay connected with others on this equation.

Never have businesses been so dependent on people and never has talent management been as crucial for business as it is today. The process of developing and fostering new workers is now a strategic business challenge. Apart from compensation it is the organisation's culture that decides if the company can retain talent. If the enterprise creates an impression that it is nurturing its employees, if it establishes an environment where there is empowerment with growth and if it provides for a stress-free vertical interaction, it is headed for a lasting loyalty of its work force and an enhancement of productivity. It is interesting to find that the national intelligence organisation in India has been practising these precepts to their last detail since the times when the modern management had not yet woken up to them.

Being intelligent means being able to identify and connect with people who can help you get to your mission in life. The importance of being able to connect has produced new businesses. Mention has already been made of the companies called Capital IQ and Friendster who help to explore connection with business executives around the world. Intelligent people are able to deliver what would be of interest to a new contact of value they are meeting with by conveying, in the right words, the promise they hold out to the latter. It is for you to make yourself and your proposition interesting enough to the person you are connecting with. In the profession of intelligence a lot of importance is attached to the preparation that an operator makes before approaching a subject for the first time with the object of raising him as a contact. It is mandatory for him to acquire as much information as possible about that individual beforehand. What this suggests is that the element of keenness should exist in the conduct of all human interactions in the day-to-day life as well.

A successful life is a life of successful relationships. Success is a progressive course that you travel with others. It is not the same thing as the wealth you inherit or the 'enlightenment' that a recluse thinks he has achieved by physically isolating himself from the humanity around. Success entails action. The concept that righteous action is more important than its outcome is at the core of the widely acclaimed philosophy of *nishkaam karma* (duty without desiring something in return) that Bhagwat Gita puts forward. It is a recommendation that suggests that successful life rests on pursuit of duty and not idle meditation. Duty always involves interaction with others.

The skill of handling people can be developed through the practice of certain norms and through an understanding of the fact that human responses are often determined by cultural values and background of the people concerned. Managing people is not something that can be taught in a classroom. It is widely felt that the young people graduating from the MBA courses are strong in analysis, power point presentation and competitive assertion but weak in inter-personal skills. The education they receive creates a sense of entitlement and a preoccupation in the mind for strategy handling at the cost of the ever-important task of enhancing the productivity of the human resource they would be working with. They drift away from the nitty-gritty of having to deal with the ground realities of labour problems, local politics and floor management. The success of an enterprise is dependent on the synergy for growth that runs through the work force of the organisation. Relationships are important for setting the right internal and external environment for the company, if this is to be achieved.

A discussion on the utility of human interaction and relationships would not be complete without highlighting the increasing significance of the emergence of multi-cultural communities everywhere. A 2007 US Department of Labour report called 'Future work: Trends and Challenges for Work in the 21st Century[2]' records that by 2050, the minority groups will make up nearly half of the population, immigration will account for almost two-thirds of the nation's population growth and almost one in ten Americans will be of Asian-Pacific-Islander descent. Any company that wants to stay competitive must come to terms with diversity – inside and outside the organisation. The true challenge facing the business world is not geographical distance but cultural separations. Culture determines attitudes to work, family or leisure time and cultural diversity, therefore, has to be managed in a manner that makes it look like an asset rather than an impediment. Being intelligent means being fully cognizant of the cultural divides with which the global business has to coexist.

Global corporations are busy recruiting diverse work groups because it is good business. Diversity drives sales. The legal and moral arguments in their favour apart, diversity efforts are regarded as a necessity for the reason that they can unleash untapped power by facilitating the generation of new ideas and innovation. This happens because of the dynamics of multiplicity that, once established, contributes to stability in the long run. Analysts believe that creating an inclusive company culture that values and respects individual difference, is likely to yield tangible bottom line results. No wonder nearly 80% of Fortune 500 Companies now have some kind of diversity staffing in place. This trend is likely to establish globalization as an inclusive phenomenon that would be successful only if it would work for the larger good of humanity and not capitulate to narrow and exploitative capitalism or economic imperialism.

The human aspect of life in business, profession or any competitive environ becomes crucial because no two persons are equal in every respect. Moreover, a human being is conditioned by his personal upbringing. He may be situated differently at home and at his place of work.

A peon may be a respectable father and a CEO may be a miserable husband at home. The personal situation can affect the performance at work. Trying to handle the other person with certain sensitivity about his or her human situation is part of an intelligent conduct. The aim should be to get every one to produce his or her best - not just as much as somebody else might have been able to do. Being intelligent means being able to make a winning team by remembering that it is working together that works.

An Intelligence organization banks a great deal on the ability to create durable human contacts. In as much as this is a requirement for success in any sphere, it is useful to enumerate the three basic approaches to human interaction that members of an Intelligence outfit bring to bear on their dealings with others. First, they always take into consideration the other individual's personality traits in any interaction. They are aware that different people need to be dealt with differently. Secondly, they know the importance of a personal conversation, designed to establish a bond by exploring areas of common interest, presaging any work related discussion. Whether it is the new customer, a new team-mate or a subordinate who has just joined the set-up, establishing a rapport with him is important. People are quite willing to talk provided right questions that would interest them are asked to break the ice. You have to express interest in a person before expecting him to get interested in you. An Intelligence man is trained in the skills of conducting an interview. He is a good listener who allows the other person to talk but while permitting the flow of conversation retains control of the interaction. He is able to study the body language of the other person to get at what has been left unsaid by the latter. Finally, an Intelligence officer never finds change disconcerting. For him no two operational situations are ever the same and he is quite prepared for such an experience. In fact if two experiences were absolutely identical this would arouse his suspicion. The moral of the story is that the environ is never static and that the men who strive for success are aware of this. For most people change means uncertainty and an avoidable hassle. For an average mortal routine is a source of stability and security. For an entrepreneur change signals an opportunity. Being intelligent means being able to grasp correctly the equation between stability and new ventures.

Endnotes

1. *Never Eat Alone,* Keith Ferrazzi, Currency Doubleday, NY-2005.
2. Business break through.msn.com, July 9, 2007 'Diversity pays off for everyone', by Joanna L. Krotz.

4 The Power of Authenticity

Knowledge is power only if the facts and data it draws upon are of unimpeachable variety. In these days of misinformation and deception an intelligent person does not move on guess-work and rejects gossip unless he thinks it is necessary to look into a rumour that suggests a fire behind the smoke. It is interesting that people who are credulous never look powerful. Intelligence by definition is information that is reliable and significant. It is important to have the ability to sense what can be taken as a corroborative indicator and then quickly accept or reject the information at hand. Information savvy people are ready to accept only authentic information and are prepared to go some length in seeking confirmation of the facts they think are crucial to their strategic planning. The pace of movement of information is fast and the time frame in which it can be acted upon for best results, is short.

The risk of acting on wrong information can cause a long lasting grave damage: the failure of an otherwise sound project produces only a short term setback. It is the authenticity of information that makes a difference between a decision and a guess. It is the power of authenticity that keeps you in comfort. People who command power always prefer authentic opinion to the best guess. The information revolution provides immediate access to thousands of sources for minimal cost but the inter-net also provides everybody the opportunity of becoming a source of information himself- trustworthy or otherwise and sharing an opinion or a whim with the entire world. This has made reliability something that tends to be inversely proportional to the volume of information.

Effective people always appear authentic in their words and deeds. Reliability is one quality that everyone seeks in a boss or a subordinate and this is associated with a dimension of character set by the individual's fidelity to the truth. It is the base of authenticity on which objectivity, impartiality and even forgiveness is founded. It brings the joys of being genuine. An intelligence organisation is a good illustration of how an entire enterprise is powered by authenticity. The cost of failure resulting from action taken on unsubstantiated information is too high in the context of national security, to permit any compromise with the highest standards of reliability. The essence of this is applicable also to the business world where decisions based on credible information are a prerequisite for success.

Authenticity involves living in a completely integrated fashion with one's values and principles and deriving there from a sense of purpose in life. Taking care not to be driven by falsehood and accepting information whose credibility has been established, is a part of living authentically. Any other life style can lead to chronic anxiety and despair. Authenticity gives you inner strength and also power to deal with the world outside. Being authentic feels so much cleaner. The power of authenticity comes into play in the wider context of a recommended philosophy of life. Authenticity is in living with integrity, honesty and strength of character – even when no one is watching. It brings you fulfillment and originality. It gets you to do things with a sense of commitment and energy. It gives you an inner sense of adequacy and makes you intrepid.

Authenticity brings meaning to your existence. Make your personal declaration of independence by doing what makes sense to you. Many people end up doing what they think would be approved by others. Many others find it easy to accept the line that all values are relative and subjective. Integrity however, is all about your authenticity as a person.

Authenticity is undisputed credibility that establishes your authority for truth and correctness. It gives you the quality of being genuine and not corrupted. Authenticity is acquiring a new significance in the context of business. It is the pull behind the new sensitivity to quality that the buyers today bring to bear on their choice of a product or service. They want to make the purchase if the performance is meaningful in terms of the experience they feel personally. In the service economy particularly, supply and cost have been superseded by quality or authenticity of the offering. The customer buys if he can identify himself with the product, the event or the personnel behind the counter, which in turn, gives a prop to his personal image. How you are attended to and how are your queries answered–all this affects business prospects because the need for authenticity must be met. Today, large companies have to create unique value while leveraging economy of scale. They have understood that mass customization is achieved when they can produce individually unique experiences for customers that enhanced the latter's self-image. Spawning variety is not equal to customization. Being intelligent means being aware of what would influence others and with that authentic knowledge trying to bring them in consonance with you. In business, authenticity is the instrument to be used for making an impact on the customers whose satisfaction now has to be in terms of the individual's choice as to what is meaningful to him or her personally. Today the customer buys because he feels bolstered due to the authenticity of his or her acquisition.

A leader uses authenticity for advancing the cause that he stands for. He shows his authenticity by willingly accepting his people with their strengths and weaknesses and then seeking to build their capabilities. In fact an authentic leader creates leadership qualities in those who are working with him. His leadership fosters the potential of his followers to lead in action. This kind of management philosophy is practised in an intelligence organization where a member at any level or in any operation faces decision- making and, therefore, has to think like a leader. This becomes possible because such an organization runs on authenticity.

Authenticity brings in responsibility as well, particularly in an organizational setting. Good companies know their brand image is strengthened by the authenticity of the people in the work force. Creative abilities of human beings derive from authenticity and this alone should guide businesses to opt for generating real value through adherence to the truth about their products and services. This is particularly important in a situation where the people's trust of businesses and institutions is in steep decline. Authenticity is rooted in consciousness. You can be at ease with the uncertainty of the world when you realize the certainty of consciousness and get the power of authenticity that comes with it.

If two players in the same area of activity or business are peak performers they can seek a competitive advantage only in something that lies in the future. Since Intelligence is by definition a kind of knowledge that tells you what may happen in the time ahead, it is clear that only intelligence or foresight can power a player into overtaking his equally competent rivals. But knowledge is power only when it is unimpeachable and futuristic in its application. Authentic people deal only with reliable information. It is a part of their maintaining a high standard of integrity. If you have the power of authenticity 'even people who do not hire you will recommend you''.

The challenge of authenticity is that it is quite easy to talk about but not easy to have. If authenticity is hard for people to achieve, it is even harder for businesses to lay claim on. The gap between the advertiser's promise and the consumer's experience is often so pronounced that it creates an impression of falsehood about the offering. It is possible that businesses resort to hoodwinking the customer because the product life is getting shorter and innovative competitors are popping up faster than before. George Orwell said: "we have a hunger for authenticity but are easily swiped by a facsimile". Authenticity is still the most important support for a person or a brand. And authenticity of communication remains the main route to establishing the brand authenticity. Authenticity generates trust and the trust in an offering can give happiness to people even in a situation of social distress. The air raid sirens during the bombing of London in the Second World War were so reliable that when the sirens were silent people went about their business without any anxiety despite the backdrop of fear.

As indicated earlier, the power of authenticity is reflected in the new trend of consumers wanting to know all about a successful brand in terms of the information about a product's content and even about the process of making that is there behind it. The days of brands adopting secretive working practices are over; the age of information is compelling the brands to move towards greater transparency. McDonald's have been amongst the first to realize that it is their secretive distant manner that led to falling sales in UK[2]. This led the company to start a website 'make up your own - mind. co.uk' that would face the critics head on and answer all their queries. Competition in a globalized economy is making it less tenable for companies to hush up what goes on behind closed doors at their production centers. They have to accept that the consumers' demand for information needs servicing. The turmoil witnessed in the financial markets in 2008 is leaving consumers with even lesser appetite for those operating without scrutiny. The best promotion of a product is when it is based on the truth well told.

In day-to-day life it is important that you are not credulous. In these days of online sourcing of information it is necessary to remember that everything that is on the internet is not the gospel truth. To assess the authenticity of an online source it is useful to seek validation of the concerned author from an established authority on the subject. A site maintained by an organization or academic institution is more reliable than an individual's offering where the web master cannot be contacted from within the site. It is good to know how often the site is updated. Another good point to check upon is whether the site acknowledges other sources within its text itself and if so can these sources be reached online. It is good to adopt an attitude of acting only on authentic information.

Trustworthiness is built on the quality of being authentic and reliable. Reliability somewhere connects with the consistency of a measure. A process or a person is reliable if you get the same result or response for the same input. This has relevance to the reliable measurement of employee performance - usually a difficult task. A good performer will have consistency in keeping with the trait of authenticity that he has in him. This can be an instrument for establishing a performance-based compensation system in an organization.

The power of authenticity gives a new shine to leadership. Many advantages come to a leader who has the reputation for appreciating and accepting only that information whose veracity had been established. Such a leader will find it easier to get valuable inputs and feedback for organizational improvement from his men who might have otherwise not spoken up the truth out of anxiety, fear or distrust. If a leader has authenticity he will be open to getting at the facts. A leader of integrity elicits loyalty of his men when he wants the latter not to keep silent over something that needed to be talked about and reported. In a setup where truth prevails, dissent is not confused with disloyalty. A leader without power of authenticity is bound to loose his image sooner than later.

The economic meltdown of 2008 evidently produced a huge trust deficit between the businesses and the consumers. According to the Edelman Trust Barometer released in January, 2009, trust in US business dropped from 58% to 38% in one year[3]. Observers believe that if the companies did not address this problem the economic turn around may be delayed indefinitely. There is talk of 'rebuilding trust' as the people seem to have lost their faith in institutions and the businesses upon their power of authenticity. The Business schools are likely to run into the challenge of having to alter the people's impression that their graduates were also untrustworthy creatures. The culture of transparency was never more in need of revival than it is today. The culture of internal transparency practised in a classical Intelligence organization perhaps represents a bench-mark worthy of being emulated as a management approach. Here nobody compromises with truth for flattering the boss and a complete freedom prevails internally to question assumptions even though the organization does not communicate with outsiders.

Leadership is a quality that cannot be borrowed. One essential quality you must have to lead is to be your own person and be authentic in every respect. An authentic person understands the purpose that he has before him. His relationships foster trust. And his value system is not marred by ambiguity. It is the power of authenticity that gives a leader an intrinsic quality of being courageous in the face of adversity and being successful in taking decisions in unfamiliar situations. Authenticity requires self-discovery. We have to continue to discover ourselves and reach that happy equilibrium with our inherent values to feel authentic about ourselves. The more you understand yourself and your motives the more strong you will feel within yourself. The power of authenticity derives from an understanding of the self in a major way. The power of authenticity does not always mean that you should be able to act strong. If authenticity brings you courage it also gives you courage to be human and to be yourself. The power of authenticity will help you to be in sync with the others in all the four domains of your life-work, home, community and self.

You may be authentic without words but when you do speak, choose words that represent what you truly mean and what you truly are. The power of authenticity comes into play in a big way in deciding the content and style of your communication with others. If you are authentic you would be aligned with your message and possibly be in no need to dramatize what you are trying to convey. Basically it means you believe in everything you say and everything you do. The more authentic you can be the more people will like you. For the same reason they will buy your products if you are in business. Remember, there has to be a link of integrity between communication and action or delivery.

As already mentioned, power of authenticity is rooted in knowledge. Superior knowledge gives you the ability to influence both people and surroundings and this is what power is. When there is a bomb scare and the bomb detection squad arrives on the scene, everybody listens to its chief because the knowledge of how to de-activate bombs puts him in a position of power. Power is a state of mind that comes from a feeling of being in control in any situation on the strength of awareness. In Intelligence parlance knowledge is power. Intelligent people fully understand this.

The roots of authenticity lie in your consciously being able to eliminate the gap between what is going on and what you think is going on. In intelligence the very first step in any operation is to test the reliability of information that you propose to act on. An intelligence organization works with people whose professional competence has been tested by its leadership. The organization can ill-afford to have any member in respect of whom there is a lag between his actual competence and the ability he presumes he has. Some of this is made up through intensive training in the special skills that constitute the intelligence trade craft. It is extremely important that an intelligence functionary first establishes the veracity of information at hand and does this in an objective manner. He must grasp and acknowledge any gaps that exist in the information he has accessed and seek to close them. He should never hesitate - for reasons of ego or anything else, to admit what is unknown to him so that he can accommodate the need for suitably modifying his operational course once some further facts come by. Remember, you get empowered in your pursuits only when you are accurate in terms of the facts or reality that you are going after.

Some people believe 'money is the measuring rod of power' but the power of money has to reckon with the power of authenticity. As a Jewish proverb puts it– 'with money in your pocket you are wise and you are handsome and you sing well too'. But money cannot buy lasting relationships, which are rooted in honest feelings sustained by the integrity of character. Just as is the case with human beings, authenticity speaks for a product too. As already mentioned the best promotion of a product is when it is based on the truth well told. Reliability is the sure source of competitive advantage. If you combine integrity with excellence you will be praised at your back. You become authentic when you are able to act as a witness to your own thinking and action. The power of authenticity cuts down ego because ego is an attitude that germinates from lack of self-confidence. When you think without ego you discover your true strengths and weaknesses and working on them, achieve progress that is real. The power of authenticity generates self-esteem and makes you aware of your own worth. A person with self-esteem establishes a positive environ around him during any interaction with others whereas a man with ego creates negativity. There is something false about ego, which causes failure. On the other hand self-esteem drawing upon the power of authenticity, facilitates success.

If you have authenticity you will respond and not react to any situation. Response is what you show when you are in control of the circumstances around you – this sense of control coming from an awareness of your own strengths and weaknesses in relation to an adversity that might have cropped up in the environ. Reaction is basically a thoughtless move originating from lack of self-confidence and is often a spoiler of success. Response is traceable to self-esteem that in turn is rooted in the power of authenticity and self-esteem is the biggest antidote of the fear of failure. The opposite of self-esteem is ego and it is no surprise that all 'reactiveness' is egocentric. While self-esteem is a quite awareness of one's own worth, ego is an edifice built on untested assumptions that drive one to desire something undeservedly. A remarkable feature of the classical Intelligence organization is the success it is able to achieve in training its personnel to steer clear of egoistic reactions. This becomes possible because all moves in Intelligence are based on knowledge, awareness and assessment and have the power of authenticity behind them.

Endnotes

1. *Confessions of Shameless Selfpromoters,* Debbie Allen, Roli-Books Pvt. Ltd. 2002.
2. *The Economic Times,* Oct. 22, 2008, 'Out in the Open', Gemma Charles.
3. *Harvard Business Review,* June, 2009.

5 The Effectiveness of Differentiation

One of my bosses who guided my work in the initial years of my career in Intelligence Bureau always said: 'there is no substitute to reading' and the significance of this dictum dawned on me the day he sent down a sixty page report in the evening for me to examine it and give my evaluation comments on it - all within the next 45 minutes. I went through the document with attention and sent it up with a terse remark to the effect that the report 'had no meat'. The boss took only a minute to send it back to me with thanks saying that 'now I do not have to go through it'. The point is that somebody had to read that report. You cannot reject information without examining it. If you have the ability to separate the substance from the chaff you can be complemented for being intelligent. Effective differentiation is a prelude to decision making.

To be able to distinguish 'essentials from nonessentials' is the running test that marks out intelligent people and defines the core competence required for making progress in any walk of life. This connects with what Vilfredo Pareto, the 19th century Italian sociologist enunciated in his famous Pareto's Law that said: 'there are a significant few amongst the insignificant many'. We do come across many well-meaning people who remain totally absorbed in the process of accessing and accumulating information without getting down to the task of evaluating it or giving out their mind on what they think of the facts presented to them. They are the ones who may run into the disorder called 'information overload' that could paralyse their output completely. Effective people also know when to stop assessing and move to decision-making. Being intelligent means taking this tough call even without total information and not letting a multiplicity of options keep you from initiating action. If you are intelligent you can anticipate even the unexpected often by putting yourself in the adversary's shoes and trying to think as the devil.

In an intelligence organisation a certain degree of informality marks the vertical interaction because whenever a challenging situation comes up, collective wisdom is invoked. There is an entire body of men, high and low, responding to the call of accountability rather than expecting a mere head or the boss to send down solutions. They generate action not power play and do not work for blind compliance. The group handling a given task has one thing in common - everyone knows what is relevant to the mission at hand. Bending together in action mode enhances the output of any team that shares a mission and an intelligence organization proves it.

Effective differentiation precedes decision making and hence it is a part of the matrix of leadership. Leadership is more a matter of aptitude than specialization. It is tested when the challenge is to work in a situation of acknowledged uncertainty or risk. This requires nerves but the ability to see what is important and what is not greatly helps. To lead means being inclined to step into the future. Intelligent people shed procrastination as this causes regression and retain initiative because they know there is no forward movement without it. Being a potential leader they chose to act not whimsically but on the basis of awareness and knowledge.

Intelligent people have a sense of the relativity of things. They can distinguish between a major problem and the minor irritants. They can visualize the long term implications of a situation or event for they can see the whole picture more easily. They can pickup information that signals an unfolding development and foresee the system or process of which it is a part.

A test of whether an enterprise stands for effective differentiation would be to find out if it has defined its strategy in intelligible terms and got its members to understand the perspective with which the organisation is working. If a member can express the mission and the methodology of the firm in a few words the enterprise is heading for success.

Corporates are learning to transit from a traditional mindset to the new age thinking by effectively differentiating between the comfort of the status quo and the promise of the future. Personnel policies are fast changing as the 'human resources' are seen as 'human capital' and the notion of training being an incentive or bonus for performing employees is now accepted as a strategy of making the human asset an instrument of growth by upgrading the skills.

Differentiation is a thought process and like in many other areas of human behaviour this may be affected by cultural nuances. This has a bearing on today's global scene where corporate environment is being rapidly place. The CEOs and the managers have to be savvy about cross-culture scenarios because interpersonal relationships are vulnerable to misunderstandings arising out of belief systems, predispositions and social values. If the handling is not marked by the right sense of differentiation, it might impact on the bottom line. A Canadian posted in an Indian metropolis while going to his work by an auto-rikshaw asked the driver if there was a good church near by. The driver told him that he knew of a famous church that was on the way to office. The Canadian said 'good' and kept quiet. The auto driver drove him to the church and waited for the foreigner to come out. The Canadian was upset that the auto driver had wasted his time and come to the church instead of taking him to the office. Here, the foreigner wanted some information for his future use. His culture said that if you are asked a question you give a reply and that is the end of that conversation. The Indian auto-rikshaw driver presumed, because of his cultural grooming, that the Canadian wanted to go to a place of worship before reporting for work. He was only being helpful[1]. Neither got what he wanted because effective differentiation was lacking on both sides due to presumptions imposed by culture. Only free minds have the objectivity to differentiate effectively.

A multi-cultural team can be a powerhouse of creativity and innovation or a place of discord and unpleasantness. The visible behaviour and words may be culturally influenced and may have to be correctly interpreted. An intelligent person should know that while diversity is a challenge, it could also be a big asset if only we harness it right.

It is now widely believed that leaders are not born but are made and that leadership qualities can be acquired and developed by people who are intelligent, who understand the human psyche and who have the drive to forge ahead. Being intelligent, they know that leadership symbolised the effectiveness of differentiation. It is again Pareto who said: 'a few govern the many'. At one level he was enunciating the idea of the elite always ruling others but he was clearly acknowledging also the fact that leaders had special qualities that set them apart from the general mass. In my own view the basics of what defines a leader in our times can be summarized in the acronym 'DRINK'[2]. A leader has to be a decisive person. His decisions are in the nature of considered verdicts and not the product of a whim or some inborn 'charisma'. He is intuitive only in the sense that his intuition represents a higher form of intelligence. A leader has to be a reliable entity, trustworthy in the eyes of those who would take his guidance. Some leaders are known to have exploited the blind trust that the followers often repose in them and in many cases they did get exposed eventually. Initiative is the visible mark of leadership which creates the environment for everyone to feel that he or she is moving ahead. Initiative is particularly tested in an atmosphere of change because only a person who can lead change will retain his initiative in the face of shifts. Initiative requires anticipation and is often tested in the willingness to take the un-chartered course. A leader does not rest on his laurels. He is setting the direction and exploring the possibility of accelerating action, all the time. The letter 'N' is for nerves that represent a synonym for courage not in the physical sense but in terms of a determination to pursue the course of action against odds and face the challenge with equanimity. And finally a leader takes knowledge-based decisions. Intelligent and well-informed people are understandably a natural choice for being given leadership roles since they are different from others.

Having a sense of differentiation comes as a boon, at every step of the life for those who want to succeed. To decide when to start taking a decision on the information that has been gathered, to delineate what is of immediate importance from what would be significant in the long term, to understand what is inclusive and what is sectarian, to avoid mixing ego with self-esteem, the subtle with the obvious or the effort with the result and generally to distinguish essentials from non-essentials, are the crucial matters that test a person's wisdom. And wisdom is nothing but applied intelligence. Wisdom is the yardstick that determines the optimal mix of intelligence and action based on effective differentiation.

A good idea will bring in results only at the end of its implementation. It is the time that separates a plan from its fulfillment. That both knowledge and time are precious resources is not really understood by many. There are 'dynamic' people who are always in the midst of a lot of activity without ever moving forward in any direction. They are seeking loads of information but not getting down to making use of all that is already at hand. They are analyzing all the time without moving towards decision-making. They have the problem of differentiating between 'time' as a valuable commodity and 'ideation' as an important asset. In my career in intelligence one of my distinguished seniors said 'we can't have too many artists in our line' and then went on to add how art was best defined as 'the conquest of substance by form'. In intelligence it is the substance that matters in all situations.

The most vital differentiation in any line of work or business is what draws a line between the strategic and the tactical, between the detail and the overview and between the 'short term' and the 'long run'. This lies at the core of being intelligent. The Indian woman, the housewife has it in her and that is what has kept the Indian society going-on intelligent savings made from small earnings. In the area of decision making I cannot help recalling that the Prime Minister whom I served as Intelligence chief once enunciated, at the end of a crucial discussion in a plenary meeting, that taking no decision was also a decision. He was effectively differentiating between a 'decision' and 'action'.

A global mindset considered so important today, basically represents the quality of visualizing the larger dimension of which an event or a local development is a part. It has the ability to see the goings on at the micro level against a macro perspective and not to let what is in the immediate, affect the course of progress that lies in the long range. This is effective differentiation in play. It is somewhere comparable to a good contingency response to an untoward incident in which, before anything else, the area of impact is quarantined to ensure that the rest of the functions and operations of the enterprise are not halted. Effective differentiation is built into disaster management where it is an aid to keeping your endeavours focused on the larger mission.

A new dimension of globalization is the sociological compulsion it creates for rising above narrow divisions of cast, colour and sect so that the best talent can be tapped for business and in fact for advancing any mission of universal application. Politics is fueled by socio-cultural fault-lines but economics assimilates these divisions for the common goal of growth. Moreover, getting involved in smaller identities detracts from the advantage of securing the whole and reaching the higher realms of knowledge. In a remarkable observation on the Indian thought, Henry David Thoreau, the noted American philosopher (d.1862) said: 'whenever I read any part of the Vedas, I have felt some unearthly and unknown light illuminated me. In the great teaching of the Vedas there is no touch of sectarianism'. It takes courage to be agnostic but to become a cause for divisiveness of humanity in the name of God is perhaps the most unbecoming form of sectarianism. Unfortunately this is the most prevalent form - causing most of the violent conflicts today. Becoming a victim of this is against being intelligent because it is an obvious insult to the very basic sense of differentiation that a person ought to have for making progress in life. Globalization has sharpened the disabilities that sectarianism can cause to any enterprise.

Effective management of knowledge is the key to handling risk. Fundamentally, risk management is about dealing with the complexity inherent in the trade-off between return and investment, using organizational knowledge for the benefit of the firm's stakeholders. In today's fast moving and highly competitive world, knowledge and learning are increasingly becoming a prime source of sustainable advantage. Organizations realize that it is no longer enough to leave critical knowledge sitting passively in the minds of individual employees. Work force mobility, the rapid rate of business change and the falling educational standards are already reducing the prospects of the employees becoming a consistent source of feedback and useful insight for the firm. The knowledge trapped within the employee base has, therefore, to be leveraged through an organizational effort to access and synthesise it for the overall advantage of the enterprise. The informal techniques of yesterday for managing tacit knowledge - the desktop, the hallway conversation, the memo, the trade show and the company get-togethers, are no longer sufficient in a scenario of radical and rapid change. The effectiveness of differentiation would come into play at the time of formulating processes that could prove most suitable for managing tacit knowledge available with the employees of different traits and placements.

Effective differentiation is relevant also in the context of a business organization trying to set its product or service apart from the competition, on a positive note. By identifying and availing of specific opportunities that permit such a differentiation to be made, a firm can achieve competitive advantage. An effort to understand what customers might have on their minds while using a particular product, can help an entrepreneur to bring out an innovative offering that scores over that product. In early nineties Oral B's managers developed a line of tooth brushes called the Indicator line by using a method of dyeing the center bristles of the brush blue to use this as an indicator. The advice was that when the blue dye gets leached away, it was the time for the consumer to change the brush. Customers welcomed this facility, which enabled them to take better care of their teeth. The company charged 15% more on this line of brush and this turned out to be a major win[3]. Perceiving an opportunity that rests on effective differentiation goes with being intelligent.

It is the effectiveness of differentiation that gives a firm the ability to distinguish what is really a new product or information from one that is not. It saves it from the trap of 'imitation'. In the nineties Sharp created an inter-divisional development team composed of as many as 14 division members, which worked to produce the electronic organizer called PA 7000 that became a huge success. The team knew that effective differentiation leads to an honest appraisal.

Today, effective differentiation provides a valuable input in decision-making. At every step of the way in life and in business you face intangibles that are felt but cannot be quantified for the purpose of analysis. Consequently decision-making is less informed than what it could possibly be[4]. You are always in need of finding the value of immeasurable commodities like the employee's morale in an organization or the impact of socio-political spectrum on the competitive environ. You cannot measure the cost of failure of information that was required for action in a critical area like national security. This is why governments spend liberally on security. Being intelligent is an index of your success in being able to measure the intangibles. It would be a major gain if the direction of impact of an intangible were determined even though the extent to which things would go might remain indeterminate. Intelligent people have a measurement orientation because it is part of their habit of accepting what is imaginable and credible.

An important application of Pareto's law in analysis is that all variables are not crucial to decision making though they may all have relevance to the course of action adopted. A few of these will be important for decision-making and others would be more for storing information in relation to the context in which the decision is being made. This differentiation makes for effective handling of the task of decision-making and paves the way for timely action. Today business decisions are taken against an overflow of facts and data and to pick on the right inputs for making the right decision one requires a logical and incisive mind that traces the core of knowledge discarding all that belongs to the fringe. Being intelligent means being able to see what is important and what is not in a given situation.

Effectiveness of differentiation is important for distinguishing the important from the unimportant in any real-life contingency and in fact in any situation of decision-making in general. It is the sense of discrimination that can help you stay calm and to accept what is unavoidable. Effectiveness of differentiation can be tested by the success that one achieves in not letting his or her personal ego become a spoiler. To be able to differentiate is a measure of maturity. It is a function of being well-informed. Good differentiation upgrades your understanding of the situation around you. It is fostered by a conscious effort to look at things from a higher perspective. It is then that you grasp how many of those things seemed inconsequential. Not only will you not mix apples with oranges, you will also rise above hasty misinterpretations, avoid wrong deductions about 'success' or 'failure' and avert feelings of instability typically caused to a credulous mind. Differentiation improves the quality of your endeavours to reach a goal and guards you against the pitfalls of envy, greed and desperation. You stand tall when interacting with your superiors and counseling your own men. Being intelligent is synonymous with being effective about differentiating between numbers, facts and situations.

If you can determine what really is the priority and release yourself from everything else, it is a lot easier to follow through on what is important. Effectiveness of differentiation can be invoked profitably in all spheres of life. It helps you to distinguish, for instance, between attitude and aptitude, pity and self-pity, and customer satisfaction and revenues. The winner's edge is all in the attitude not aptitude because it is your attitude that would determine how you act. Pity is one of the noblest emotions but self-pity is possibly the most ignoble. Lexus established itself as a best practice company by tying the compensation to its dealers to customer satisfaction not to revenues.

Nike registered great success through ads that focused not on the product but on the customer's needs and wants. It sent out its sales force to spend time in the field with the people who love and play a sport and then built a marketing strategy around their enthusiasm for that sport. Nike made good use of the effectiveness of differentiation when it claimed its shoes must have souls. It may be mentioned that an Intelligence organization always judges its performance from the success of the professional skills used in its projects and not just from the quantum of results achieved. An exposed operation can cause more harm than a failed one - a differentiation that is so crucial in the context of an intelligence outfit.

Being intelligent means being able to differentiate between 'brilliance' and 'application', between the 'plan' and its 'execution' and between the 'destination' and the 'journey' that must be undertaken to reach it. What marks a successful 'application', 'execution' or the forward movement of a 'journey' is persistence. It is erroneously presumed that persistence is tested only against odds or in a situation where you face some huge or impossible tasks. The fact is that persistence is a measure of the mental strength that is needed to put in an effort in pursuit of a goal, by consciously taking time out for it as much and as regularly as possible. You can become a Piano player within a timeframe provided you practice on it for a time regularly. Successful authors write a few pages every day. Persistence is doing a thing on a note of positiveness and not reducing the work to a burdensome act. One of my bosses always reminded me that one should 'never neglect the routine'. He was commending a habit that could be fostered by 'persistence' and that would contribute to success. It is rightly said that winning is a habit. And persistence is a major differentiator as far as creating new habits is concerned.

As already mentioned, Pareto's thesis that 'a few govern the many' translates into a great socio-political reality of our times inasmuch as everywhere it is an elite that is managing to rule the large masses and that too in the name of democracy. In the professional and business fields, there is the rise of the brotherhood of the strong against the relatively weak. Moreover, globalization seems to have induced the trend of an alliance of the big businesses consciously aiming at achieving dominance of the world economy in their segments. In this some of them from the developed West could even be working out an understanding with the political elites across national boundaries in the developing world and altering the concept of sovereignty itself to create a new form of hegemony. In all situations whether global or local, it is the effective differentiation between the potentially powerful and the relatively weak that is made by an intelligent person to his advantage. At the same time one should be aware that the concentration of wealth is already creating swathes of unrest across the world. Violent protests at the mass level and insurgencies are witnessed in many parts of the globe. The spread of the Maoist movement in India is an illustration of the impact such a development can make on the strategic environment. An intelligent entrepreneur sees the importance of the atmosphere of public trust and goodwill around his enterprise. He can effectively differentiate between the short-term gains and the sustainable profitability in the long run. Being intelligent means having the ability to see the line between the apparent and the real, between the journey and the destination and between the tactical and the strategic.

An intelligent person steers clear of any false sense of prestige or egotism when it comes to yielding to the demand of a course correction. A smart firm knows that it can win not by waging a corporate warfare but by seeking negotiated advantage and accommodation. It backs its moves with good intelligence. Globalization has brought Corporate Darwinianism into play and smart people know that this will favour survival of the fittest-not necessarily a victory for the strongest. Competition is in the minds not in the muscles and this differentiation comes naturally to intelligent people. Businesses with more funds and workforce may be vanquished by smaller players who acquire a competitive edge through a smarter execution of their strategic plans.

Effectiveness of differentiation helps to save time, energy and expenditure. If you can provide the same service at a greater speed the customers will be attracted to your business. In today's world the convenience of queue jumping that gives a user the feeling of having saved some energy, becomes more attractive than a discount. Of course, retailers seek to differentiate themselves by discounting prices all the time. In tough times the ability of brands to differentiate themselves from the competition, holds the key to success. Differentiation is in fact, at the root of good customer service that provides competitive advantage in business. The entire utility of software in improving delivery is based on the effectiveness of differentiation.

The ability to differentiate is linked with the ability to put right questions and see the nuances in the answers that apparently looked the same. Knowledge is power because it leads you to right decisions and this happens because knowledge gives you the ability to differentiate better. The power of differentiation therefore comes from being well-informed. The ability to differentiate gives the ability to innovate and intelligent persons know this. A form of intelligence test has been developed by Collin D. Ellott, called the Differential Ability Scales (DAS) to distinguish between individuals on the basis of their intellectual strength in the area of differentiation. Researchers have tried to measure the techno-conceptual ability of the individual to observe, learn and apply and also to keep track of the feedback on his action. The effectiveness of differentiation is the essence of intelligence and hence the backbone of success.

An emerging facet of the effectiveness of differentiation is concerned with the understanding of the importance of the sense of urgency in day-to-day life. Any organization, if it has to become a high performing entity, must make a conscious effort to uphold the value of time as an organizational resource. This will happen only if its members realize that working with a sense of urgency is required even outside of emergencies. If the enterprise is doing well it is easier for its personnel to fall into a sense of stability, contentment and complacency. Those who are intelligent are aware that we live in times when change is all around us. Intensity of competition, technological breakthroughs, the ongoing globalization, the pressing need for innovation and the unfolding of new knowledge, are all combining to accelerate the rate of change. An ingrained sense of urgency can keep you from falling into the mindset that tilts towards status quo. Such an inclination can prove to be the undoing of all prospects of progress and success, today. Urgency helps to enhance productivity per unit of time even when there are no pressures. You will find people who are averse to the idea of working on an urgent footing confusing the sense of urgency with doing things in haste. It is good to try to be conscious about carrying out a task without wasting time. In the current environ of an economic slow down, one way of avoiding waste is to enhance the awareness about making every moment productive. Urgency, moreover, must become the instrument that carries you towards the goal and not remain merely 'a matter of doing things with speed'.[5]

Endnotes

1. *The Hindu, Business Line,* Delhi, June 16, 2008.
2. *Intelligence-A Security Weapon,* DC Pathak, Manas Publications, Delhi, 2004.
3. *The Entrepreneurial Mindset,* Rita Gunther and Ian Mcmillan, Harvard Business School Press, Boston, USA.
4. *How to Measure Anything,* Douglas W. Hubbard, John Wiley & Sons Inc, 2007.
5. *A Sense of Urgency,* John P Kotter, Harvard Business Press, 2008.

6 Analysis is the Soul of Intelligence

Analysis converts information into intelligence and intelligence into strategy options. Collating facts, examining them for their significance and putting them together like pieces of jigsaw can lead a competent analyst to a view of what is on the anvil. Since analysis defines the agenda for action it is clearly a leadership function. In any professional organisation or business concern the analysts should operate under the direct care of top management. The process of analysis may unravel gaps or flaws in the information content and the analysts therefore have to have the authority to call for more data from within the organisation or outside.

Being intelligent means being observant and being observant means taking cognizance of whatever is noteworthy in the scene around. The ability to discriminate between the important and the relatively unimportant in any situation is linked to the skills of analysis. An analytical bend of mind gives meaning to being intelligent. Analysis in fact is the soul of intelligence because it is built into the process of interpreting information and initiating a knowledge-based decision. A good analyst has to have all the traits of an information savvy person. He is never disabled by excess of information. He likes to establish reliability of the facts before accepting them and does not hesitate to question the veracity of the source that has furnished the information. He can rise above the mere detail to grab the substance of the data and conclude even when there is some paucity of information.

Those who handle analysis must be broadly aware of the sources from which information has come. This helps them to evaluate the credibility of the information and also to fix the direction in which search for a collateral confirmation could be made. In a well-run firm the analysts should be empowered on behalf of the decision takers to question the people who had furnished information, for any gaps and contradictions noticed in it. They should also have the freedom to go to the leadership to point out any mismatch that they had discovered between information and the action initiated on it. That is why successful organizations have easy vertical interactions that are not subjected to excessive bureaucratization. An intelligence organization establishes a benchmark in this regard.

The merit of good analysis is linked to the analyst's capability to steer clear of certain pitfalls. The most important aspect of analysis perhaps is to be objective in examining facts. Often we allow wishful thinking to creep into our findings. Insufficient examination of a situation or an inference reached in haste, are flaws that detract from a competent analysis. It is not correct for an analyst to seek shelter or comfort in vagueness and take recourse to generalization in the absence of the required information. Suppressing the negative signals emanating from the analysis or ignoring information that is entirely new or too different from what had so far been factored in, just because it is not fitting into the picture envisaged, can lead to serious damage or harm to the organization. The gravest pitfall of the analysts is the tendency to report what would please the masters.

As the Scottish philosopher Thomas Reid said: 'there is no greater impediment to the advancement of knowledge than the ambiguity of words'. A good analyst records his findings in a language that is precise and clear. He neither underplays what is potentially unfavourable nor exaggerates what is rewarding. However, even as the findings have to be unbiased, rooted in facts and marked with clarity, they should always be recorded with emphasis so that they do not miss the attention of those who will use them for decision-making.

Analysis involves application of human mind. Tools like Automatic Textual Analysis and Synthesis do help transform raw data, heterogeneous in terms of the source and language, into information. Today analysts have the advantage of using multi-lingual text mining techniques to get an overview of great volumes of textual data but the final results of analysis depend entirely on human intervention.

It is said that the left side of the human brain is analytical and the right is intuitive. The first step in analysis is to pick out facts or statistics that are relevant and significant. One then puts two and two together to see if any pattern emerges that indicates what lies ahead. Analysis for intelligence is meant to delineate an opportunity that can be pursued or indicate a risk or threat that would have to be averted. The intuitive competence of the brain basically is in the area of anticipation, in the ability to foresee what lies even beyond the pattern that analysis has established. Analysis and intuition are both functions of intelligence. They take you, from the present into the future. Intelligent people dwell into the future dimensions of any situation with ease because they are attuned to looking ahead.

Analysis presages action. Good decisions usually have systematically assembled data and analysis behind them. Intelligent organizations use statistical and quantitative analysis as a propelling tool. This is integral to information-based strategy that an enterprise has to adopt for forging ahead. Today analysis-based decisions are universally regarded as superior to moves made out of an individual's whims and fancies. The importance of intuitive decision-making remains because it connects with intelligence. The noted Indian philosopher J. Krishnamoorthy aptly describes intuition as the highest form of intelligence. Intuition in fact is rooted in knowledge that has been assimilated and sublimated into the thinking process. In recent years poor decisions of global import have been taken with calamitous results. The decision of the US President to invade Iraq, General Motors collapsing because of its wrong decision about which cars to bring to the market or the Time Warner running into a problem because of its decision to buy AOL, have been widely cited as illustrations. Is this because decision-making is viewed as a prerogative of individuals? 'Information goes in; decisions come out - and who knows what happens in between'.[1] In a successful firm decision-making is focused around systematic analysis. The age we live in demands knowledge-based decisions. Intelligent people realize this.

In business, analysis is a major instrument for generating actionable intelligence. It comes into play both in project formulation as well as in its execution and adds value to them. Analysis helps to decipher 'predictive models'[2] that drive decisions. However, one of the transformational impacts of 9/11 was that it shifted the emphasis from the mathematical model of analysis of the available information to the 'case scenario method' of taking the unpredictables into account.

Good information management depends a great deal on the capabilities that have been created for integrating data and finding new meanings in information. The objective is to facilitate decision-making. When computer application to analysis first came into use in the 1960s it was appropriately called 'Decision Support System' (DSS). Today, the world's IT infrastructure is facing the danger of crashing under the pressure of a trillion strong collectivity of devices, objects and processes and the people using them. Some relief is promised by the new model of services called 'cloud computing' in which processing, storage, networking and applications are accessed as services over networks. It is the success of an intelligent system that vindicates my belief that knowledge comes in integral packages. A comprehensive analysis of the 'package' alone can yield intelligence that would lead to the right decision for the future. IT software, can only supplement, not supplant the human skills and intelligence that analysis is anchored on. In the globalized world, assessment of the competitive environ, evaluation of the home advantage of a firm and the estimation of the likely response of the customers to a product are some of the vital areas where a finding can be produced only by analytical brains. Developing skills of analysis should be a part of all human resource development programmes in the corporate world.

Today, no business can hope to get an edge without making a competent analysis of the competitive environ and taking control of the environmental issues affecting the enterprise. Businesses have to move beyond litigation and the pressure to keep up with regulatory change. Analysis should be able to bring out options by using imagination for pre-empting the possible fall-out of the negative features that exist in the scene outside. In today's world a sound strategy has to integrate a multiplicity of determinants that set the competitive environ.

It may be mentioned that security failures at the national level are known to have occurred not because of the lack of intelligence but on account of wrong analysis and assessment. The Independent 9/11 Commission in the US faulted the intelligence analysts for showing the 'group think' syndrome while handling the information on Iraq and producing a tailored report. Psychologists describe 'group think' as a condition in which the desire to produce a unanimous verdict overtakes the regard for facts and objectivity. A project failure sometimes results from lack of action on the analysis report simply because the findings in it had not been able to adequately draw the attention of the decision makers. Results of analysis therefore must always be presented and communicated loud and clear. The main purpose of analysis in fact is to produce findings that can be used by policy makers.

A successful analyst has to have critical thinking. He does not hesitate to raise questions on the credibility and relevance of the information that comes to him for examination. He would do well to remember that analysis ultimately helps to take correct decisions. Insightful interpretations add value to analysis. These come to those who are aware that the purpose of analysis is to generate the best options for moving ahead. Analysis is the bridge between information and action.

Good analysis is required for making the right strategic

moves in situations that entail due diligence, vendor verification, assessment of the political scene, evaluation of risk in a new geographical location and reading of the market. Accurate data and competent analysis can enable a start-up company to get the better of the competition. If a smaller player has better decision-making tools, it can surprise a stronger rival by just being bold and put a bigger player used to only incremental shifts, on the defensive.

Most successful organizations now have an enterprise-level core establishment to act as a 'business intelligence competency center' or BICC. Among other things it ensures that fruits of analyzed data are made available throughout the organization. There have been many instances of a single analytical initiative resulting in large savings or revenue increases. Business analysis has emerged as a most important facet of applied intelligence. That is why no business executive or manager can be successful unless he has three traits in common with competent analysts– an instinctive reliance on credible information, an ability to distinguish the significant from the unimportant and a logical mind that raises the right questions in any situation.

In a fast changing world, a new challenge is to conduct analysis in a matrix of uncertainty. Analysis is a process that helps you to look ahead on the strength of what you know. The inevitable element of uncertainty that a changing scenario introduces in all decision making, strategy planning and project execution in these times, is testing the ability of business leaders. Because of the significant proportion of assumptions that one needs to make in addition to the knowledge that has become available for decision-making, conventional planning is yielding to adaptive planning which allows room for testing assumptions. Accordingly, analysis has to cover not only the existing reality that is established by knowledge but also take into account the creatively enacted patterns that could be projected by 'imagination'. The risk of testing out assumptions has to get incorporated in business planning. This becomes an imperative in situations where new information emerges piecemeal. Even marginally reducing a previous state of uncertainty is important[3]. Today, a rolling plan seems to be the appropriate strategy for all entities. This approach to strategy is traditionally followed by national intelligence organisations that have to be open to receiving new inputs on threats and extending their plans to deal with them.

Good decision-making is anchored on competent analysis. It is an index of the importance of analysis that companies are now beginning to outsource decision-making and benefiting from this. With a shortage of analytical skills in the United States and Western Europe and a ready supply in India, Eastern Europe and China, it is perhaps not surprising that organizations had begun outsourcing these more cerebral functions. The trend began quietly in the mid-1990s at General Electric's captive off-shore center in India.[4] Today several off-shore firms specialize in decision analysis for their clients that include some of the largest US-based companies.

In a situation where the decision making may have to do with less than a complete looking information base, it is important that you take a view on such facts as are available, in their totality. Key decision makers should be able to visualize and synthesize the picture after ensuring that no information was left out of the consideration. The existing approach to management education is compartmentalized and this makes it inherently inadequate for enabling the trainee to keep pace with today's fast changing business scenario. Moreover, we are overtaken by a sort of technological civilization that demands rapid and radical changes in our approach to various issues. Business management programmes must therefore connect with technology, design and innovation. An intelligent mind, which necessarily will be an analytical mind too, has to be ready to meet this challenge. In fact thinkers, politicians and businessmen, all 'need to sense deeper, communicate clearer and act faster'.[5] They have to be aware that in the absence of analysis they may run into unintended consequences of their actions.

You have to understand your business but also, more importantly, you have to have a deep understanding of the people concerned with it. Intelligent people know the importance of cross-disciplinary learning. They can be innovative about their solutions because they are able to look at the human, social and psychological needs of their work force, the users of their services and the potential customers waiting in the wings. Their analytical mind helps them to see the emerging unarticulated needs and realities and to think of new approaches to meet them.

In the final analysis, being intelligent means being smart and being smart means being quick with analysis. Bill Gates said in one of his interviews: 'smartness is an ability to absorb new facts in real time to get an insight'. An intelligent mind becomes an analytical mind whenever it is engaged in just seeing, reading or even thinking. Today IBM's motto is: 'a smarter business needs smarter thinking'.[6] The company claims that its powerful computing models and advanced analytics will enable businesses to move beyond simple sense and respond capabilities towards prediction. Using information to make smarter decisions and to apply the right insights to the business in hand, is the new mantra of the corporation. Being intelligent means being instrumental in making your organization smart through the application of an analytical mind.

Endnotes

1. *Best Practice,* Thomas H. Davenport, *Harvard Business Review'* Nov. 2009
2. *Competing on Analysis,* Thomus H. Davenport, Harvard Business School Press, Boston, 2007
3. *How to Measure Anything',* Douglas W. Hubbard, John Wiley & Sons, 2007
4. *Harvard Business Review,* Feb. 2009
5. *Businessweek.com,* June 15, 2009
6. *The Economic Times,* Delhi, March 10, 2009.

7 Imagination is more Important than Knowledge

When Albert Einstein said that 'imagination is more important than knowledge', it was not a scientist treading into the realm of philosophy but a man of intelligence advancing the frontiers of rational thinking. Being intelligent of course means being well-informed, in the sense of being fully abreast of what is happening in the present but it also means developing the ability to visualize what can happen in the future. Imagination is not some wild illusion but a sense of anticipation that one brings into play while examining the facts in hand. When an analyst reads the picture revealed by the jig-saw pieces put in place, it is the imagination that helps him to see beyond the immediate scene and make credible deductions for the future. Imagination adds value to analysis. It is a combination of the rational deduction from the data and an application of forward thinking to add insight to the interpretation.

Perhaps the most important case in recent times illustrating this is the report of the Independent 9/11 Commission in the USA that clearly faulted the security analysts there for showing a lack of 'imagination' in evaluating the intelligence that was available before the attack on the Twin Towers. The Commission noted that the US Intelligence had the information to the effect that elements belonging to the Al Qaeda were already there on the American soil preparing for a hostile act, that they were planning to hijack domestic flights and that they had surveyed the tall buildings of New York. The Commission expressed concern that the intelligence analysts did not logically proceed to examine all the possible scenarios of the Al Qaeda carrying out its threat. Vital bits of information apparently went unnoticed such as the report that some Arab youth taking lessons at the simulating machines of the flying clubs showed a distinct preoccupation with the technique of taking off without showing any keenness to know about the skills of 'landing'. Nothing stirred the imagination of the security establishment with the result that the warning of an impending attack of Al Qaeda contained in the famous August 6, 2001 memo of the CIA was dismissed as old history, at the Principal's meet.

American intelligence had not imagined that suicide bombers were planning an attack using hijacked planes as missiles. The unbelief of the people brought up in the 'rational tradition' about a motivation that can make young people so willing to embrace certain death, is reflected in the recent book[1] of Walter Anders of Alabama University. The book revolves round the question as to whether rational agents can carefully prepare and execute a plan of action that calls for their own demise.

The importance of anticipation being built into intelligence assessments was again highlighted in the context of the Madrid train station bombings on March 11, 2007. It was said that imagination could have helped to initiate some preventive endeavour about what turned out to be the 9/11 for Spain. It should have been possible to anticipate that since skyjacking had been rendered too difficult and too risky after 9/11, terrorists would be thinking of targeting a weaker link like the railways.

Imagination is behind all creativity and since imagination is also a facet of intelligence it can be said that an intelligent person has a creative mind. Creativity goes with an attitude of doing anything joyfully with a sense of freedom. All children are creative because they have the freedom of imagination. By and by a growing individual submits to beliefs and social codes that tend to put him under attitudinal confines. Creativity is suppressed by forced activity. Also, we are part of a society that thinks creativity is something that is going to pay. Creativity will come into play when there is freedom from fear of failure. It is not motivated by fame or money though these can come in as its bye-product. Imagination helps an entrepreneur who launches his project after deliberation but without letting any undue concerns mar his forward thinking. Imagination is anticipation and can be distinguished from a fanciful thought or day-dreaming. It is visualizing what you can do through means that are viable. Aggressiveness borne out of ignorance is not a part of it. Imagination helps to see an opportunity and sight a potential danger that lies ahead.

Intelligence and creative thinking go together. They pave the way for innovative responses to business dilemmas. Studies of highly creative artists, scientists and writers generally reveal that the latter score high on tests of intelligence. Comprehension of complexity, self-confidence and ability to resolve apparent contradictions, help creative thinking. Above all, it is the commitment to a task or the objective that propels creative thinking in a challenging situation. In turn, creative thinking is a measure of the extent to which you can change and adapt.

Innovation suffers in an organization when no one has time for ideation. Companies too often rush to production without having spent more time on creative brainstorming. The enterprise is too busy meeting customer demands, putting out fires and dealing with people. You have to treat innovation as an event, schedule it and allocate time for it. If you don't look at it with a sense of priority you may end up putting the occasional big idea thrown up by some one, on a back burner. So hold a brainstorming session consciously giving it time and attention. Intelligence planning and operations are helped by creative thinking that is developed through brainstorming sessions incorporated in the professional training programmes. Remember, in a typical brainstorming session the loudest people tend to be heard while the quieter people of analytical bend of mind tend to get lost in the melee. Do not let this happen. Being intelligent means letting a hundred flowers bloom and getting the session to generate a large number of ideas. This enhances the prospects of a gem or two being thrown up.

It is necessary to study the competitive environ constantly as this sometimes gives you an insight into a possible new opportunity. In the wake of the economic melt-down of 2008 a pint-size $ 300 device known as a net-book became popular as it cost just half as much as a traditional lap-top. Ten to twenty percent of customers who would have bought a PC took to net-book, as the latter was a light PC capable of handling web surfing, e-mail and other basic tasks. Made by companies such as Dell, Hewlett Packard and Taiwan's Asus and Acer net books have risen as the consumers have cut back. The sales exploded in 2008 to an estimated 11 million up from 1,82,000 in 2007.[2] Net-books illustrate how imagination can bring a cheaper, less capable but competitive entity into the market to prevail over a well-established product. It is said that net-book could even cause trouble to Microsoft. Net-books cater to people who spend most of their time dealing with online services and want a cheap, light device they can use on the go.

The Indian thought anchored on Vedas is a good case study of how imagination helps knowledge creation. The Vedas are not God-centric writings but a treatise on insights and perceptions flowing from the observations on how nature works and how is human existence placed in the scheme of the universe. Nothing is as remarkable in the sphere of imagination as the precepts of the ancient sages that there are multitudes of solar systems or that there is a 'universe' in the smallest particle of the physical body. The visualization of a solar system-like arrangement within the atom must remain the most outstanding empirical deduction made from imagination as applied to the cosmic patterns seen from outside. The interpretation of stability or peace as a constant accruing from intense activity or 'Karma' was likewise drawn from the insight into the dynamics of the Solar-centric universe. The Karma like the motion of the planets has to be free of personal motives and for the larger good, to bring peace and stability. The sages proved that imagination could enhance the frontiers of knowledge.

Imagination can work for countering the moves of the adversary. Recently when security concerns arose in India about possible flow of bad money into Indian companies, the government responded by initiating a revision of FDI guidelines so that security-vetting mechanisms could be put in place to fish out anti-national elements among the investors. Imagination would be on test in identifying and countering misuse of the legitimate banking channels by the malcontents.

In the information age many non-state players and even government-allied groups are engaging in sophisticated cyber spying and other forms of attack that have led analysts to project a possible next world war as a cyber warfare centered on the disruption of critical national infrastructure systems. Targeting of air-traffic controls, financial markets, water and sewer systems, electric supply and even traffic lights could be expected. Media recently referred to a White Paper of China that claimed that 'informationised armed forces' would be a part of its military strategy[3]. Intelligence assessments on security against such threats will have to invoke imagination or anticipation of a high order.

Considering the unsatisfactory crime situation in many regions and the rise of the mafia with its adverse impact on the industrial and corporate life, it is not difficult to imagine that security at the work place is acquiring a new importance. Beyond the universal need for protection against commercial espionage, subversion and sabotage, a business enterprise today stands to make a long range benefit from security orientation and awareness of its personnel. Training programmes in this sphere would help to bind the members of the corporate body together and also strengthen their perception that their own security and well-being lay in the safety and economic strength of their enterprise. If security management becomes a part of the corporate management, it would be easier to encourage punctuality and discourage unauthorized absence on the grounds of security that are understood by all. Security has thus acquired a strategic economic significance inasmuch as it can become a factor in enhancing production. In a modern setting security management should be made more inclusive. Security promotes loyalty particularly if it were to be projected as a contribution of all those who cared for the organization. Today, security, welfare and loyalty constitute an integral package.

Imagination is the base on which organized professional groups forecast demographic and other trends about the society's future. It is predicted that as genetic testing and other medical break-throughs become available widely, aging population will increasingly outsmart chronic diseases[4]. An intelligent forecast in business is about the rise of the so-called 'cooperative consumption'. As technology for pooling demand and resources increases, highly sophisticated sharing even beyond national boundaries will come into vogue. Time- sharing at holiday resorts is already a big business worked out only through imagination.

Beyond knowledge it is imagination that creates the ability to see things in the larger perspective, something that is so essential for sound decision making. Man is the only creature blessed with the sense to distinguish the macro from the micro and take the 'bigger view'[5] of a thing or an event. Noticing the small detail and juxtaposing it with the big picture thinking, is at the base of an intelligent response. The perception of the bigger dimension is somewhere linked to an understanding of the larger goals and higher values. It always gives you better options of response and action.

Seeing things in the larger perspective is an acquisition that comes with adulthood and is a sign of growth. It not only makes for the correct interpretation of what you see but also keeps you from overestimating the loss and underestimating the positives. Moreover, if you have a persona that cannot rise above the details, you are too obvious to be interesting. Perspective develops when you have experience, the ability to make analytical deduction and also the required spiritual quotient that fosters imagination. Experience is a gift that the past gives you, analytical derivation concerns the handling of information in the present and imagination bolstered by spiritual quotient makes it easier for you to perceive what lies ahead. Seeing things in the larger perspective means having an integral view of the past, the present and the future. It also often helps you to tide over a set back that comes at the end of an honest effort because you can place it just as a part of the bigger scheme of things.

Innovation is an offspring of imagination. Emergence of IT based lobby banking that enhances bank's profitability by reducing rentals and staff costs, is a good example of imaginative innovativeness. Sophisticated automated consoles run on next-gen software is enabling the customers to carry out many banking transactions themselves. The new ATMs accept cash, count it and check for fakes. They use advanced identification systems including biometric scanners. They not only save on space and staff costs but also provide a platform for beaming advertisements. This is a win-win situation for both, banks as well as customers[6].

Innovation is doing new things. When ideation or creativity is put into action and tested for viability it turns into a successful innovation. In the age of knowledge thinking up a new thing and implementing it can lead to a business success. Toyota is known to have made good use of the enormous power of production workers to detect a problem and suggest solutions. In 1980, the number of adopted suggestions per thousand workers in Toyota was fifty times more than what was happening in General Motors[7]. This accounted for the vast amount of innovation in Toyota's factories and improvement in their performance in the US automobile market. Intelligent people are likely to be creative too and they can by their imagination generate ideas and set off the innovation process. Smart organizations are beginning to garner collective intelligence also called the 'wisdom of the crowd' by providing an environment that would work for cognitive diversity by facilitating the viewing of the same content through different lenses. They would make way for a suitable degree of decentralization in content management so that there was freer interaction with content within the organization and the crippling effect of the corporate guidelines seen elsewhere was not allowed to come in the way.

Innovation needs insight and sometimes insight comes like a flash. The German chemist August Von Stradonitz Kekule was so absorbed in deciphering the molecular structure of organic material that he dreamed up the Benzene ring - the basic building block of aromatic compounds. It is said that in his dream he found atoms dancing like snakes and saw one snake forming a loop and eating into its own tail. That imagination of his, conjured up the hexagonal ring of Benzene. Creativity comes to a mind that pushes on in a logical progression and this makes it a bye-product of intelligence.

In a case reported some time back, imagination was what led a set of young entrepreneurs headed by one Avinash Garg, who had spent some time in the US, to start a website for users in India called Route guru.com. They saw the need to provide a detailed description of the route one must take to reach a destination in the shortest possible time. The USP of this service is that it describes the land-marks on the map together with point-to-point distance in kilometers so that one could reach one's destination without having to ask passers-by. In the Indian conditions the land-mark based route guidance should prove a particularly useful idea. These entrepreneurs used imagination to steal success out of the monopoly of Google with its bench-mark search-engine[8].

Another example of imagination in business is the growing online tutoring which is already a $ 4 billion industry and is growing at an estimated rate of 10-15 percent per annum. The world-wide market for online tutoring is estimated to be in the region of $12 billion. In a country like India online support is more affordable than regular tutoring[9].

Entrepreneurship in fact is deeply connected with innovation and change. An intelligent person is an entrepreneur at heart because he is capable of thinking differently and is in the quest for a solution all on his own. The Grameen Bank model of the Nobel Laureate Dr. Mohammad Yunus of Bangladesh, rested on the thought - and he was thinking differently – that the poor people are credit worthy. The Grameen Bank is said to have kept the rate of defaulters to almost nil[10]. Entrepreneurship is an aspect of how to convert an idea into action. It is a mindset that goes with being intelligent. Today, success in business is determined not so much by liquidity as by the use of intelligence for creating new products and business models.

In business, imagination of what would fill a need of the customers can yield a new line of service and a competitive advantage. Domino's was not the first pizza chain in the USA but it was the first that promised home delivery and that too within a specified time limit. This gave it a distinctive edge and set it apart from all other such chains. The Domino's used the knowledge about the consumption of pizza as ready food for families to foresee the importance of a quick home delivery facility and organized business focused on that consumer benefit. Nearer home Tata Motors, the leading producers of commercial vehicles, took the innovative step of creating a new product category called the 'mini truck' – a four-wheel small commercial vehicle in the sub-ton class. The produce called Ace sold over one lakh units within a period of 22 months from its launch in 2005[11]. The company made an intelligent use of the knowledge that in India the roads and highways were improving and that a smaller cargo vehicle could make faster and easier deliveries in small towns as well as in the interiors of large metros where entry of big trucks was regulated.

Using imagination National Geographic recently got into video games and opened a subsidiary NG Ventures to work with game publishers to turn its material into games for PC, consoles and hand-held devices. It believes that its content is extremely well suited for a global gaming audience. Here imagination was used to create knowledge-based products. Of a similar class was the initiative taken by the search giant Google Inc in November 2008 to push the internet war to a new high by launching SMS based service that will offer search facility across the country at cheaper rates to those who have mobile phones but do not have internet connections. Of the 300 million mobile subscribers only 5 to 10 million mobile users use a data plan on their handsets. The next 100 million are savvy SMS users and it is for this segment of the market that the SMS search was created. Users can send a search query through a text message to a service number and expect to receive an automated response with relevant results[12].

Innovation becomes easier if knowledge can be demystified by asking the right questions about the why and how of a process and its product. Right questions help to refine the training tools and get ordinary people to do extraordinary things. Today the focus is on capacity building in the sense of making the work-force more productive through on the job training. Apart from improving on what has been done in the past the thrust of advancement is also on unraveling the untested turf by exploring any signals that may be pointing to the latter. Curiosity, questions and imagination draw you closer to these signals.

Innovation is also aided by the integral packaging of knowledge. Apple's I-Pod is an interesting example of this. It stole the thunder out of the MP-3 music players by combining its exclusivity of looks and ease of use with the facility of connection to an online store where you could legitimately buy music and download it to your instrument. I-Pod became an economic product by integrating revenue stream from two sources – the hardware cost and the stream of sales of music.

Of the same class is the convergence of the mobile communications and Internet industries, which is opening up new growth opportunities for both these sectors. Noting the demand for richer mobile experience, Nokia recently unveiled OVI - a platform for its internet services that would include a music store and games. The company is foraying into internet communities that would like to have on-demand music and games. Combining communications with entertainment content is expected to advance the growth of what is now established as the multimedia business. While focusing on the mobile phone market Nokia has developed innovative product features with imagination and has made India its second biggest market after China, overtaking its market in the US.

Nokia has taken advantage of the fact that knowledge admits of integrated packaging of internet services that technology is laying the run-up for. The company has worked on the anticipation that in a new market like India, the mobile phone for many people will be their first screen. Their first experience of the internet, of video calling or of e-mail will be through a mobile device and not a PC. Nokia rightly foresaw that mobility combined with the access to the internet would bring about a paradigm shift in the life style of the people at large particularly if the mobile device could also become a navigator. In the world of tomorrow your phone could be your wallet if ATM could be operated on it.

It is not difficult to imagine that in the coming years the mobile phones would become a media option for users to access information that is available through TV station or the Internet. There is a likelihood of the mobile operators developing their business on the lines of a media company and delivering, for instance, insights to markets. This is going beyond the limited mobile marketing and beyond the status of mobiles being just a communication system that lets you download music and some other entertainment. Once mobiles become a medium for more than 300 million subscribers who are there at present, it can become an advertising platform of substance impacting on the whole pattern of budgeting of companies for advertisement.

Sometimes transformative changes occur in business and lifestyle due to small shifts. Businesses were critically affected when glass bottles gave way to plastic bottles, card board packaging of tennis balls shifted to metal cans and the tetra pack made it possible for small town shops to keep fruit juices on the shelf for days together. When the semi-conductor chips moved from germanium base to silicon in the eighties, giants like Hughes and Cleveite producing germanium were shaken up and overtaken by a tiny company like Texas Instruments using silicon based technology. High reliability and lower costs made this transition epoch changing, drastically altering competition and the position of leadership in the industry. Innovation is the product of an environment where the status quo is constantly challenged in a bid to seek change for the better. It is a paradox that the more successful a business organization becomes the harder it is for it to accept change. IBM in eighties was a leader in every market it chose to serve but the era of PCs knocked the profitability out of its mainframe computing.

Innovation in technology, design and media are transforming both consumer cultures as well as the business cultures. There is a welcome trend of innovation being driven by the thought of the benefit of society and the humanity at large. A bye-product of this trend is that markets are looking for cost-effective ways of reaching their audiences so that dependence on high cost traditional media can be reduced.

Most major companies have Chief Information Officers whose role is fast changing from being the providers of assisting or enabling services to becoming the creators of business model innovation and generators of revenue earning products. Mainstreaming of the IT specialists into the top management that handled strategy, is a trend that has already set in. We are moving into a world where knowledge production and power will be in a confluence to ensure that value creation happens fast. The traditional corporate hierarchies would be broken as the driving force of the company will be the harnessing of the vast amount of knowledge through collaboration across cultural and geographical boundaries. IT revolution will anchor a deepening global inter-dependence. Its forward march cannot be reversed because it contains the promise of sustaining economic growth and raising global living standards. Knowledge sharing is graduating to a conscious pooling in of imagination as well. It is clear that even competitive instincts will not be able to obstruct this trend driven by the larger will of the humanity.

The economic melt down of 2008 has brought in the importance of imagination in newer ways. Intelligent firms have tried to mitigate the sense of distress of their work force by educating them about the nature of the unpredictability facing them. It is good to give people as much information as you can about what will happen and when. If shocks are preceded by fair warnings, people not only have time to brace themselves but also get chances to breathe easy. Again, it is not difficult to imagine that in a situation of downturn of economy and the turbulence it has created, a very important part of driving efficiencies is to proclaim a 'war on waste'. Hindustan Unilever Limited recently announced that it had established cross functional teams to identify and put in place actions to eliminate waste from the business.[13] It seems distress can activate imagination; the saying, 'necessity is the mother of invention' comes to mind. Intelligent people not only have a spirit of inquiry to know more, they also have the curiosity that propels them to explore new grounds by applying imagination.

Endnotes

1. *The Political Economy of Terrorism,* Walter Anders, Cambridge University Press, 2006
2. *Business Week,* December 8, 2008 , McGraw Hill
3. *Hindustan Times,* Delhi Nov. 30, 2007
4. *Hindustan Times,* Delhi Nov. 30, 2007
5. *Getting Things Done,* David Allen, Penguin Books, New York 2001
6. *Hindustan Times,* Delhi, November 30, 2007
7. *Managing for Innovation,* Watts S. Humphrey, Prentice Hall Inc. 1987
8. *Economic Times,* Delhi, Nov. 20, 2007.
9. *Hindustan Times,* Delhi, Nov. 28, 2007.
10. *Hindustan Times,* Delhi, Dec. 6, 2007.
11. *Economic Times,* New Delhi, 21, April, 2008.
12. *Hindustan Times,* New Delhi, November 19, 2008
13. *The Hindu- Business Line,* Delhi, July 4, 2009

8 Communication is the Key

The ability to observe, absorb and analyse needs to be complemented by the skills of communication that link information with action. Good projects sometimes fail because of inadequate or flawed communication in the matter of intimation of the decision itself or in the sharing of instructions about the implementation. Communication also is a prime determinant of how interpersonal relations get shaped and what benefits one could possibly derive from human interactions. Intelligent people make sure they are never misunderstood and by raising the right questions and making the right interventions they also ensure that they have correctly grasped what the other side was trying to convey. Information is shared through transmission. Tacit knowledge can remain unutilized unless it finds expression and that is why an intelligent enterprise finds ways and means of establishing a sound system of internal communication so that, among other things, the objective of knowledge creation within the organisation is served.

Communication is the base on which all human relations are founded. Communication serves one or more of the three basic purposes - explaining what your stand is in a matter, presenting what needs to be described and defined by you to the others and trying to influence the view point of another person. This covers most situations in life at work and at home though sometimes in a private setting, silence becomes the best medium of communication. These facets of communication roughly correspond to your interventions with your seniors, your direct reports and your peers. The three fundamentals of proper communication are helpful in each case and they deserve to be enumerated here. Clarity of expression comes first. What you communicate should not lead to more than one interpretation. Secondly, brevity should not be at the cost of clarity. And finally, there should be a logical sequencing in whatever you are communicating. Commands that go wrong are almost always in violation of one of these three requisites of good communication.

Communication broadly is of two kinds - face to face which is something not always possible to have and through some tele-link or the internet that is becoming the most common mode in both personal and professional realms now. Face to face interaction is the most credible, direct and effective communication as both sides do not lose time in achieving the right understanding of the matter at hand. Electronic mail as a medium of dialogue with an individual or a group is pretty quick, effective and marked by clarity but it does not offer the opportunity of interpreting the body language that so often becomes necessary for getting the best results in an interaction. It also does not factor in the importance of listening and responding that often is the most important part of communication available only in a face to face meeting.

Communication gives the best results when the communicator maintains his cool while presenting a point but conveys to the other side his own commitment and sense of urgency towards the project or task being described by him. In dealing with the points of clarification raised by the other side, impatience or anger should not be allowed to seep into the tone or the choice of words because this will never go unnoticed and will inevitably impact the setting in which the communicator is trying to achieve his objective. No two persons talk about or perceive a thing in an identical manner and this itself makes communication a skill that is unique and demanding of perfection. Since 'knowledge is power', it is the communication that rightly becomes the instrument with which to wield this power. Exercise of power entails an interaction with others. If you are leading a project or a team your communication also is the key to having an effective control of the situation.

It is the quality of communication from your side that will determine your success in garnering knowledge that you are seeking from others. Good communication opens up a two way flow of information and an intelligent person uses a sprinkling of right questions to keep up this flow. This is how he can even access the thinking processes of the other side and evaluate the strategic direction the competition was likely to take. In the profession of intelligence the capacity to influence the understanding of the individual you are interacting with and drawing him out is a valuable skill that helps an operator in cultivating a contact or ferreting out information from an unconscious agent.

Talking of the importance of brevity in communication, Twitter where all messaging is restricted to 140 characters may be bringing back the art of saying things short, simple and succinct. You should be able to convey the most complex ideas and themes in 140 characters if you are a smart communicator. The whole discourse of public debate has become so verbose that it is killing the interest of the citizens in all that their politicians say day and night. Successful leaders in public life stay connected with the people on the strength of their ability to transmit their ideas and values in simple short expressions.

How you communicate with others largely determines your success in getting along with them. This applies even to your own personal world. What your mind tells you is happening to you and what you communicate to your own self is what sets your perception of where you stand. You can therefore develop the skill of communicating the positive elements to your mind even when the situation around you is beset with negatives. It is for you to interpret a failure not as the end of the road but as an effort that did not take you to the desired point. A setback could be seen and communicated as a signal for the recourse to another option and the exercise of another launch. Communication is necessary to set things in motion and movement is necessary for progress. Remember, experience is what you get when you do not get what you want and that is a gain too. Competent communicators are able to reach the mind of the other person and get him or her to understand what you are trying to convey. Moreover, a good communicator also manages to read and assess the responses of the other side not only from the spoken word but also from the body language. Preparatory moments are needed sometimes to bring the others on a common grid with the communicator's mind. This is important in conferences, board meetings and even in public speeches. Smooth and effective communication needs a common wavelength at the two ends.

Communication works for organizational coherence and unity particularly when the company's manpower is thinly spread across geographical stretches. Technology has eliminated 'remoteness' and helped to make linear organizations more slim and viable. It has made the corporate bureaucracy a little more accountable. Communication can rise above language barriers and smoothen the working of a company operating across cultural boundaries. Good communication can ensure that your employees can be heard and understood regardless of the language barriers. Communication is the instrument with which you can reach out to the people on the 'front lines' and make your values known to all those who are working for you. If you are a leader you should be able to explain in two minutes where does your organization have to go.

It is the facility of instant communication that has enabled the successful corporations today to consider the world to be not only their market but also their factory. A company might manufacture a complex product by combining high-tech automated assembly in the US with labour-intensive assembly in an Asian country or the Caribbean. It may run a production line that has a thousand mile gap and an airplane to bridge that gap. Today micro-wave and satellite communications make it possible for state side and off-shore production managers to communicate easily. Even drawings and designs can be electronically transmitted. Globalization has made it possible for the companies to combine the best resources from around the world – all because of the communication revolution.

Since the human mind works on the logical progression of thought a business enterprise which is in essence a collectivity of men and women, has the immense backing of the organization's denominational strength of logic. Intelligible communication on which the inner efficiency and health of a corporate body are based, is nothing more than a logical transmission of ideas. For an organization being intelligent means establishing an internal grid of logical understanding among all its members through a system of communications in which nothing can be misinterpreted or misunderstood.

Today's managers are required to act as enablers rather than enforcers[1]. In this changing role communication skills become very important. In today's world understanding relationships is the key to managerial success because relationships are not authority driven but communication driven. Unless there are compulsions of 'restrictive security', policies should allow all employees easy access to colleagues who can help them carry out their tasks speedily and efficiently, regardless of their status or area of operation. This also helps knowledge creation. Good managers are also successful handlers of human networks. They need to focus as much on overseeing employees 'below' them as on managing people across functions and disciplines.

Observation and absorption require concentration of mind. The mobile and high-tech age may be making people adept at 'multi-tasking' but one of its greatest casualties is our ability to focus on the matter at hand. For instance, to be in the present and be attentive to the colleague or client whom we have engaged in a conversation in the course of work, is not as easy as it sounds. We like to respond to e-mail messages during meetings or while on phone. In the process we are talking to someone but thinking about something else. Allowing minds to drift can lead to loss of information and the loss of an opportunity to meaningfully connect with others. Managing distraction is becoming a specialization on which a new kind of business of coaching is being created. A San-Francisco based firm, Mariposa Leadership and

Illinois based company called Dare to Engage work on the idea that attention can be bolstered through training[2].

Lack of communication is one of the most frequently cited complaints against managers. It is through communication with the leader that the team members learn their goals, understand the tasks they are to perform and get to know of how their performance has been viewed. If this communication link was weak the total outcome would be deficient. Good communication has to be a two-way interaction. The leader has to make sure that he has been understood. He also needs the feedback that would help him bring about an overall improvement. Miscommunication or lack of communication can potentially lead to disruption and loss; it can surely create an environ that encourages rumours and internal rifts. Participative management sustained by good communication between the manager and his team members, creates a cohesive and productive team. This kind of management brings in the best results at all levels. The need for communication becomes even more important as you go up the vertical hierarchy because management at the top levels has to progressively rely on top down communication that is backed by a system of feedback travelling up to the corporate apex.

Intelligent organizations make investments in establishing an efficient system of internal communication. One of the greatest problems in a large organization is the paucity of vertical interaction and to makeup for this, communications must be kept free of the possibility that they would be modified or amplified to a point of having been corrupted all together. Communication is vital to engaging people in the enterprise. Goals and strategies must be communicated clearly, concisely and consistently to all employees. People have a tremendous capacity to handle the truth and respond well to challenges. What they cannot handle well is rumour and the uncertainty it creates[3].

Communication forges strong relationships that in turn generate trust. And trust is the key element that defines good business transactions and personal dealings. Further, we are in an era where wealth is the product of knowledge. Information, consequently, is the most important competitive weapon of our time. The unintelligible intellectual capital is the sum of everything everybody in a company knows that could give it a competitive edge. Communication is the only effective tool of management for handling the knowledge worker and turning the untapped and unmapped knowledge of the organization into a competitive advantage.

It is the technology of instant communication that has brought about the transformational shift from the old 'process' of production in the industrial age, with its notion of a set time and place to work, to the new capacity of a worker being able to operate from anywhere in the world. Communication is the basis on which Japanese manufacturers have been able to do away with stockpiles by ensuring that parts were delivered just in time. In effect they did this by substituting information for inventory.

The key to effective communication is simplicity. Good communicators take something complicated and make it simple. Ronald Reagan became a great leader because of his uncanny ability to communicate. If you want to connect with people keep it simple and forget about impressing people with big words and complex sentences. If you want to become a better administrator become audience oriented. Every time you speak to people give them something to feel, something to remember and something to do. Do not just dump a bunch of information on people. Remember, you are a leader only if there are people following you. And this will happen only if your communication creates in them a sense of connectivity with you. Intelligible communications are nothing more than a logical transmission of ideas. Such communications are easy to understand because they are always worded in a simple idiom. 'Simplicity is the ultimate sophistication'.[4] An intelligent organization succeeds because it establishes an internal grid of logical understanding among all its members through a system of communications that leaves no scope of misinterpretation.

You can seize only what you can see. A sensible vision is, therefore, the most important element behind any successful transformation. It is through communication that the vision is made visible. The most carefully crafted messages rarely sink deeply into the recipient's consciousness after only one pronouncement. Our minds are too cluttered and any communication has to fight hundreds of other ideas for attention. A communication not understood and absorbed would be a waste. It should, therefore, be accepted that effective information transfer almost always relies on repetition. Being intelligent means having the competence to restate a point or formulation in a subtle way and ensure that what you communicated was understood at the receiving end.

Endnotes

1. *The Book of Hard Choices*, James A. Autry and Peter Roy, Morgan Road Books, New York, 2006.
2. *Hindustan Times*, Career Gallery, Delhi, September 16, 2008.

3. *Strategy for winning employee commitment*, Douglas S. Sherwin, Harvard Business Review on Management, 1975, Harper and Row, New York.

4. *The Power of Simplicity*, Jack Trout, Tata Mc Graw Hill 1999

9 Intelligence is Information for Action

In the profession of Intelligence the classical test applied to an information of intelligence value is that it is something that would call for an immediate response or action. Action follows a decision to adopt a particular response option and defines the end use of intelligence. Being intelligent therefore means that you not only have knowledge but that you put it to use for your progress. If you have intelligence and you do not act on it, you are not being intelligent. Of course, your conscious decision not to respond is also an action. The point is that you have to be pro-active about acquiring knowledge and following it up with action. Any action needs time. This is what makes knowledge and time such precious resources. All cultures uphold the quest for knowledge and decry idleness. You may run into a big failure or loss if you had the intelligence or knowledge that called for a remedial action but still you did not initiate a timely follow up. The risk is not in moving too quickly and going out of control but in moving too slowly and going out of the running.

National security can be jeopardized if the nation's Intelligence agencies do not get the right intelligence or if they have information but fail to pass it on without delay to the action taking authorities. In either case the enemy might succeed in executing his nefarious plan. The most unfortunate cause of national security failure, however, would be the one where the authority or the State had the intelligence but failed to act in time. Failure of action is perhaps more serious than the failure of intelligence. There are cases in world history – and in the experience of our own country as well – when failure on either count caused serious damage to the national interests.

Action on information is not retrospective; it is always what you do from now on. Intelligence logically is information that gives you a capacity to do something for the future. Being intelligent means being in a position to utilize knowledge for a futuristic decision-making. Knowledge of the past is important as history. An intelligent person moves beyond what has already happened, taking the best lessons out of the past. Knowledge of what happened in the past has its value but intelligence is for handling what lies ahead. Being intelligent means being successful in using knowledge to foresee an opportunity or an impending danger. Being able to convert information or knowledge into intelligence by analyzing what is there in it that could lead to some deductions, is a manifestation of being intelligent. The same facts may be available to everybody but an intelligent person has the capacity to pickup the important from the unimportant and put it together to read a new meaning in those facts. Intelligent people have an analytical bend of mind.

Being intelligent certainly means being knowledge savvy. This refers to the mental capacity to note and retain meaningful facts without clogging the mind with unnecessary storage. Knowledge savvy individuals seek out information and predictably tend to accept authoritative opinion, discounting all guesswork. They have a logical mind that enables them to decide what they are looking for and why and where will they find it. This keeps them focused. They have a natural interest in understanding human behaviour, which helps because applied intelligence always concerns dealing with people and the society around. Above all, the information savvy individual has his bearings right in determining how to make the right use of information at the right time.

To act or not to act is one cruçial question that crops up ever so often in our lives and we end up either acting on inadequate examination of the situation or prevaricating till the time for action that would give us the best results, is over. Inaction is the outcome of the fear of failure, lack of awareness or an inborn procrastination. Action on the other hand lacks merit if it is taken without any thinking, under compulsion or out of fear. Being intelligent means being pro-active in the sense of being ready to push forward with action. The intelligent people know that action is the execution of a decision and never a mindless activity. They also remember that it is the four saddest words of speech that constitute the expression — 'it might have been'.

A basic requirement of being intelligent is to avoid thoughtless action. Ralph Waldo Emerson said - 'the ancestor of every action is a thought'. Conscious action involves some kind of decision-making which in turn rests on the knowledge that is relevant to it. We seldom realize that in any effort, big or small, the first step has to be a thinking to define the desired outcome. It is rightly said: 'begin with the end in view'. It makes sense to set out on a journey with the understanding of what the destination is. Much of our daily activity is a routine affair and unless we are careful it can rust the urge to think in a focused manner about getting the best results from an effort. Few people feel they need to preserve and develop the habit of increasing their productivity. 'Outcome thinking' is one of the most effective means of turning wishes into reality[1]. Thoughtless action can lead to unintended harm and can cause a loss of both time and energy. Planning presages purposeful action because it involves thinking. This is the stage that allows for the 'out of box' contemplation. Whether the action is a response or a new initiative, thinking or planning must precede it. Even the response to an emergency requires effective thinking.

An upshot of being thoughtful in action is that one has to remain mindful of the unfinished business. This is necessary to ensure that action is pursued till its logical conclusion. A system of reminders helps to take a lot of load off our mind. Such a system may involve practices ranging from calendar dates to sit down reviews. The ultimate quality of a responsible person is the ability to finish.

In today's competitive world you have to take a decision at every step of your life and a simple recipe that greatly helps you out in this is to develop the inclination just to do the right thing. 'Do what is right and you will never go wrong'[2]. You can resolve the most difficult and entangled issue by remembering this simple advice. If you are in the role of a leader you must seek continuous improvement in the output of your team. A healthy attitude of being in a state of continuous dissatisfaction with the existing state of affairs helps to drive the process of upgrading the system at hand. In the management of an Intelligence organization this ethos is built into the conduct of all operational work. Such an organization adopts another important plank of leadership: it gives freedom to its members but does not mix it up with autonomy. Being intelligent means being aware of the fact that the centralization of decision-making and delegation of the responsibility of execution can go together.

Being intelligent means being pro-active about moving ahead. Once you are clear about the desired outcome you should get started. Justifying putting off the task does not help. Unless not responding is in itself a conscious decision, there is no reason why appropriate action when called for should not be initiated straightaway. Emotions should not be allowed to suppress the will to act. Results are achieved not by invoking luck but by investing in purposeful work. Remember, all this is easier said than done. Many people formulate plans all the time but do not implement them. Sometimes they miss the boat just because of prevarication. Importance of action was perhaps best described by late Dhirubhai Ambani, founder of the Reliance Industries, who said: 'meeting the deadlines is not good enough; beating the deadlines is my expectation'.

Thomas Henry Huxley said: 'the great end of life is not knowledge but action'. Time is an investment and should never be wasted. There is a correlation between intelligence and the ability to keep time. Accuracy in timing activates the brain processes responsible for reasoning and problem solving. A sense of timing and understanding of the value of time make for quick and deft responses to any call for action. Both information and the time required for acting on it are precious resources and intelligent people know how to use them. Napoleon the Great famously said: 'I may lose battles but no one will ever see me lose minutes'.

Since time is a precious resource none of it should be wasted or frittered away on sub-normal productivity. One can get the best output per unit of time by remaining focused on whatever one is doing. Three things help you to get the power of focus. First, make every activity a conscious choice. Do something not because you have to do it but because you have chosen to do it. In an Intelligence organization every operation is the outcome of a conscious planning and is a focused activity. Secondly, in this age of constant inflow of information the ability to weed out or rise above distraction is an imperative if you wish to remain focused. And lastly, remember that if you are focused you are making your actions measurable and gaining a reputation for consistency, to your great advantage.[3]

Initiative is what drives a man of intelligence to take a considered decision and then implement the plan of action. Such a person is both a thinker as well as a doer. He has to have the curiosity for knowing more and while in action, the will to 'work it out'. Action is built on initiative. Initiative comes naturally to those who believe they are still to reach the top. Handling action tests the acumen for leadership. It often invokes the quality of courage that is an essential trait of a leader. Courage is the ability to act in the most fearful of situations with clarity. In such a situation, fear makes the leader's mind more focused. The leader turns fear into a source of power. While a leader has to take knowledge-based decisions he is driven by his vision, the clear and vivid picture of the future that he has in his mind all the time. A leader's decision or vision will be of no consequence unless it is communicated down the line. If a leader is decisive but is unable to communicate his decision to his men, his leadership will be on a discount. As George

Bernard Shaw once wrote: 'the single biggest problem in communication is the illusion that it has taken place'. If you are a leader your people have to know, feel and see the direction you want them to go. A leader enhances his own reliability or trustworthiness by giving those around him the training, space, freedom, authority and support. Leaders oversee their charge but never micromanage it. In a business enterprise they create a culture of exploration where everyone seeks to unlock value for his own satisfaction.

Man is gifted with free will, a sense of discretion to follow the good and avoid the evil and an inner measure of adequacy. An intelligent man uses these gifts to develop self-confidence. He is conscious that trepidation vetoes success and understands that being intrepid does not mean being foolhardy. It means being pro-active and optimistic. He knows that in the socio- political dynamics of our age, the response time to opportunities and threats has shortened. An intrepid man can hold his own, even when traversing through un-chartered waters. In today's life this could be happening frequently. Situations would come up which require competitive interaction with unfamiliar individuals and organizations. Finally, an intrepid person abides by the society's norms but has the strength to stand up to them when they cease to make sense.

If you have not failed to act, your failure is basically an effort that did not succeed. Failure at the end of an effort is to be distinguished from the failure to act. In today's fast moving world there is a certain acceptance of the calculated risk that is built into an otherwise well planned endeavour and that is why when the desired outcome is not there the intelligent thing is to try out the project with a reformed strategy incorporating suitable correctives. This is a healthy trend. A positive way of dealing with failure is illustrated by the case of the space shuttle Columbia. When the shuttle crashed killing all the astronauts on board, NASA did not abandon the effort. It examined extensively what had not worked and introduced new initiatives incorporating measures to prevent such catastrophes in the future. The mission succeeded eventually. An intelligent organization steers clear of a needless blame game and an intelligent person does not cry over the spilt milk. They do not waste any more time and move on. Success does not require any special skills except passion.

Business schools teach management principles but not the art of getting things done. They have training modules that do not necessarily prepare the students for participative management which is a prerequisite for successfully leading a team in action. Their primary focus is on how to analyse and view a problem the way a CEO or an MD would do. The courses do not cover the subject of Intelligence and its use in a competitive environ nor do they highlight the paradigm shift that information age has brought about in the understanding of such concepts as leadership, innovation and the challenge of change. They at best polish the basic talent and the intrinsic abilities of a student and give him or her a rational-looking case for building self-confidence on the strength of the knowledge stored in books. However, when you come out of the phase of analysis and step into the arena of action, you discover that all controls are not in your hands. As the competitive environ unfolds and other players show their cards, you may have to be prepared for course correction. Even for a well considered plan the execution will always be a challenge because what involves human interaction will never be totally predictable. The Business Schools cannot over emphasize the reality that all business is human activity and that to succeed as an entrepreneur, is to succeed with the people.

Decision and action always bring in the question of risk that confronts a business leader. Risk is measurable in terms of the degree to which uncertainty exists as a factor when you are taking a decision. What will reduce risk is not your experience of the past but what you can anticipate would happen in the future. In any line of business risk is indirectly proportionate to the available intelligence. Since complete intelligence is difficult to come by in any strategic area of national or business life, risk should be accepted to the extent your decision making consciously takes into account what had remained unknown till that moment. Often, important decisions have to be taken on incomplete information, in business this happens all the time. Here one can draw upon the approach adopted in the sphere of national security challenge. You keep part of the budgeting and resources apart for meeting an unpleasant surprise. Being intelligent means becoming a risk taker without losing self-confidence and optimism.

A catalyst that drives action in any organisation or business enterprise is its mission statement. The mission statement defines the goal and delineates the pathway for reaching it. Its importance lies in the fact of its being a constant reminder to everybody in the organization that there should be no wasteful diversions of energy and no irrelevant investments and that both leaders and managers ought to evaluate and audit their endeavours on the higher perspectives contained in the mission. The mission statement is designed to make what is first perceived as impossible, look possible. It gives the members of the organization the inspiration to feel that they are part of something big and important. It lays the ground for competent decision-making and efficient execution. Enron[4], a pipe line and energy company turned into a trading company in a bid to achieve faster growth but soon landed in chaos because its changed mission was not backed by appropriate reorganization of the outfit's value system and behaviour and a redefining of the processes, checks and balances.

When an action is invoked there should be a sense of urgency to sustain it. Remember, changing the face can change nothing but facing the change can change everything. It is natural for any organization to have some elements playing up skilled filibusterers in an operation. They keep action on hold while being seemingly busy in sorting out preparatory details or settling the logic of where to start from. There should be no avoidable loss of time in executing the plan. Also, what is to be guarded against is the possibility that in a team pursuit, progress is slowed down just because everyone had not been driven out of his comfort zone. Complacency in the implementation of a project is something that can happen without anybody even detecting it. To avert it the leader has to be fully aware of the need to establish a grid of urgency among all concerned about pushing ahead with every passing moment. Being intelligent means being cognizant of the line that separates confidence from complacence.

Being intelligent is to realize that you are not born effective, you become effective by adopting a progressive attitude to work and becoming a self-driven learner. One way of doing this is to believe in participative management in all situations. You would then understand that appraising and performing go together, that knowledge to be of any use has to be put into action and that work can become a means of self-actualization. Participative management fosters positive inter-dependence, which is rooted in the healthy perception that performance of a team is caused by all members. Remember, a team leader is also the energy manager, which means that he or she produces synergy in the work unit.[5] Intelligent people realize that to do nothing is to be nothing. Even spiritual advancement requires activism and that is why *Bhagwat Gita* puts forward the twin concepts of 'karma' and 'dharma' in one bracket. It is the progressive attitude to work that enables you to optimally realize your potential and move to the top of the performance chart.

A smart enterprise is led by people who know that a gap between idea and action is what causes failure in many cases. A good strategy gets nowhere if it does not move towards implementation. There should be no withholding of action out of fear of failure. Once action is on way a smart leadership makes the arrangement to acknowledge any extra effort made by the staff and to appreciate any value addition made by a performer who creates new learning. In an action oriented firm the leadership keeps the employees on board in pushing towards the company's long-term objective. It also seeks quicker results by ensuring that everybody gets to act in his or her area of strength and thus produce more in less time.

Setting targets and dreaming about them is considerably more fun than having to meet them. If people at the top tend to be target setters rather than implementers the organization is not assured of success. Imposed goals cause unnecessary stress and create fear of failure: what a successful company needs is a culture of excellence in action that brings in a sustainable competitive advantage, 'not the sugar-high of quick wins'.[6]

Endnotes

1. *Getting Things Done,* David Athens, Penguin Books, New York, 2001.
2. *Doing What Matters,* James M Kilts, Crown Business, NY, 2007
3. *The Power of Focus,* Jack Canfield & others, Health Communications Inc, FL, 2000
4. *Winning,* Jack Welch, Harper Business NY, 2005
5. *Performance Management,* Prem Chadha, Macmillan India Ltd. 2003
6. *The Hidden Danger of Target Setting,* Philip Delves Broughton (*Magazine Today,* June 2009)

10 Interplay of Strengths and Weaknesses

Right from the family in which you are born to the universal human order in which you will grow, your progress is determined by what others do to you and what you do unto others. Every step of the way that you traverse brings you the results of how you stand in relation to those who constitute your area of contact and how do the factors in the wider environment affect you and the other fellow beings around you. It is a constant interplay of the pluses and minuses of the situation of which you are a part that determines the direction and pace of your advance. An important plank of being intelligent and well informed is to have a fair idea of your own personal strengths and weakneses and those of the people and the situations facing you at any given point of time. Do not try to do every thing. See where your strengths lie and proceed to stay focused on one area at a time.

You have to reckon with other players in your line of business or profession, working on your relative strengths and fending for your vulnerabilities. Competition has turned into a combat and you have to strategically plan for your success. The climate at the market place and the threats and opportunities contained in the competitive environ have to be gauged and evaluated but over and above all this, one has to deal with the challenge of change itself. Brisk social transformation, changing job scene and the shortening product life cycles - all combine to test a person's intelligence and sense of stability. Management of the chaos is translating into every one's life. Preparedness to transit from one task or track to another calls for an even greater dependence on your capabilities and wits together with an attitude of acceptance of change. Do not see change or a surprise as a catastrophe but take it as yet another challenging situation. Make a quick count of the helpful factors in the environ as well as your own resourcefulness and invoke your intuition or imagination to take a decision. Intuition is intelligence refined by knowledge, experience and forward thinking.

Winning companies will need to know the world, its markets, its technologies and its people so that they can draw in enterprising individuals and innovators for collaboration based on complementing strengths. Competitive strengths are going to be tested out in the areas of innovativeness, intelligence assessment and the ability to work in a cross-culture environ. Taking up the last first, it is indeed an index of the hold and tenacity of cultural identities that the 21st century has witnessed a very large number of violent conflicts by way of insurgencies, cross border wars and communal discords along cultural fault-lines. This defies any expectation of greater levels of peace in the world in the post-cold war era. While this phenomenon needs to be researched it is possible that under the skies that are free of the perennial tension caused by the rivalry between the two super powers, people are seeking safety in their smaller regional and communal identities.

Well informed people are alive to the possible impact of development on the competitive environ. Induction of new technology may have to be examined in conjunction with the question of how it would be received socially. Science and Technology often leave the issues of social acceptance far behind. In 2003 a complete sequencing of the human genome, comprising six billion base pairs, was achieved and James D Watson who had first unraveled the double helical structure of DNA in 1953 became the first person to put his personal genome sequence on the internet. This immediately raised the ethical issues about how much personal generic information should be made known or shared with others as this could affect social relationships[1]. The DNA sequence can indicate vulnerability to cancer, diabetes and cardio vascular disorder. On the one hand we may move towards a healthier world but sequencing, on the other hand, could also have the potential to change the way we think about marital relationship and family that, in turn, could affect social structure itself.

An effective organisation works on the strengths of its men by getting them to do their best in what they are good at. The organization will excel only by amplifying strengths, not by simply trying to rectify its weaknesses. New managers at Toyota were made to attend a three-day Great Manager training programme that showed them how to spot the strengths of their subordinates. A good team is one in which every member concentrates on giving off his best. This is what multiplies the team's potential. Working on your strength you are likely to be more creative, more innovative and more decisive. Of course, awareness of weaknesses and an attitude of not letting them road-block advancement will help but success is achieved basically when you push forth with your plus points. In an age where awareness is the prime requisite for progress in any field of human endeavour, 'failure and success are not opposites, they are merely different'[2].

An intelligent enterprise has managers who discover what is unique about each person and then capitalize on it. They convert a person's particular talent into performance and realize that in his or her area of strength an employee will produce more in less time making an obvious value addition. In an Intelligence organization this principle of management runs through the system. Most executives elsewhere spend only a miniscule part of their time on thinking about the practices that can enhance productivity of the firm by improving on the delivery of the individual employee. A successful company focuses more on building up its collective internal strength than on remaining obsessed with discovering the strong points of the rivals through the bench marking exercise.

Globalization has confronted businesses with the challenge of launching their operations in new areas and facing consumers of diverse cultural profiles. Intelligence lies in developing the ability to ride on cross-culture bridges in pursuit of success in any field. In early 2008 Harlequin Enterprises, the publishers of the Mills & Boon series launched their business in India not only by bringing their international titles to the Indian market simultaneously with their release in the rest of the world but also by initiating a new romantic series with an Indian flavour and Indian characters in Indian settings, for global sale. Their first venture in this was a book titled 'The Virgin for the Billionaire's Taking' in which the hero is a business tycoon who also happens to be the brother of a Maharaja[3].

Businesses have to adjust to cultural imperatives that affect the responses of a society. The image of a boss, the concepts of leisure and entertainment and the value system as a whole embracing honour, cooperation and hospitality, are all culturally determined. In Eastern societies the boss at work is respected like a father figure and he has therefore to keep himself sufficiently informed about what is happening within the family of the subordinates. A 'siesta' in the afternoon is considered a legitimate right of the worker in some tropical environs. Importance of festivals, mode of displaying hospitality and the system of gifts are all cultural symbols that vary from place to place and have to be understood by the new entrepreneurs anywhere. Cross-culture mobility and awareness are needed to energize people and drive them towards the goals. Awareness of socio-cultural needs and concerns often comes in handy in resolving disagreements. It can be said that a 'localized global corporation' is the new trademark of success in business today. A flat structure, an international foot-print and a sustained programme of training the personnel for cross-culture assignments and postings are the hallmarks of such a corporation. Cross border flows of the people and capital are still to grow. Global companies need to be acutely aware of cultural differences across the world markets. Their relative strength in achieving 'localization' will determine their success. It is no surprise that diversity training is now becoming an important component of B Schools. International experience has acquired a new meaning.

IT revolution, which ushered in the 'knowledge economy' has sharpened the competition for tech supremacy. The companies are battling for software engineers who want to work for tomorrow's technology and not merely improve upon the yesterday's. The knowledge economy has in fact become the talent economy in which the collective abilities of a company's employees become its main source of power. It is now realized that a diverse team will connect better with customers who are likely to be equally heterogeneous. Corporates should build diversity on moral grounds and not merely to fall in line with a CSR.

It is the battle for talent among behemoths that resulted in the $44.6 billion bid of Microsoft for a forced acquisition of Yahoo in February 2008. Microsoft's $31 share bid came at a time when Yahoo was trading at $19.18 at the end of a series of quarters of declining profit. The impact of the bid further pushed up the share value of both Microsoft and Yahoo. The prospect of the mega merger frightened the IT giant Google, the internet search leader into launching an aggressive effort to play the role of spoiler. It cried foul and appealed to the policy makers around the world to intervene as the merger posed threats to competition. The US Justice Department and the Commissioner of Competition for the European Union indicated that they would examine the anti-trust implications of the deal[4]. The Microsoft's effort fell through as Yahoo dug in heals but the episode showcases a 'corporate warfare' in which the two sides tested each other's strength.

The advent of IT revolution has added pace to life in a manner that is making change the only constant for all of us. All strategic plans based on an evaluation of the interplay of internal and external factors have a short life today because changes in environ can happen without much prior notice. Your strengths and strong points may lose some of their relevance. Being intelligent means being aware of the consequences of change and developing an attitude of taking on change rather than skirting it. To be a leader means to lead change. Any success story, in the times to come, will revolve round this new component of leadership. In a dynamic situation a leader should be able to retain an organizational focus to which all within the enterprise are totally attuned. It is the strength of leadership that will crucially decide if a firm is going to gain and retain a competitive edge.

You take a lead because of your superior strength and not because others had some weaknesses that you did not have. Success is a product of forceful endeavour not a bye-product of being virtuous merely. It is a dividend of progress not a consolation for an averted failure. As the Chinese book of military craft says 'Your armour gives you security; your weapons give you victory'. The armour protects you against your vulnerabilities but the weapons give you the strength and the thrust to get the better of the adversary. In a world of competition you work on your strengths and try collaterally to make your weaknesses immaterial. The challenge lies in identifying your strengths and trying to sharpen them. It is not unimportant that you can define your personal flaws that detract from your ability to work to your strength. Intelligent people objectively evaluate the strengths and weaknesses of their rivals, their peers and their partners. This helps them in getting the best out of any dealings with the latter.

You will probably perform better in the areas that evoke your interest and involve you in what you like doing the best. Working on your strengths, however, is not at par with your enjoying a past time, it is a test of your determined effort to achieve results. Awareness of your strengths and weaknesses and those of the others you interact with gives substance to your effort. It helps you to see an opportunity and perceive a threat. Also, it is a part of being well-informed that vitally assists you in hiring the right help and assembling the right teams for your projects. Your strengths and weaknesses become relevant when you are in the pursuit of a goal. You cannot be immune to them unless you chose to become an inactive recluse. When you are rubbing shoulders with your seniors, your colleagues and those who work for you, you may unravel your strengths and uncover your handicaps. If you are intelligent you will lose no time in remedying your shortcomings and maximizing the utility of your strong points. You should research the origins of your flaws and analyse the setbacks of the past that could be attributed to them.

You work on your strengths in defining the direction of your business and making choices about how to focus on competing. You make your product, your service or your ambiance exclusive in a manner that no one can beat it. However, one has to remember that businesses are vulnerable to transformative technologies, innovations and shifts in the competitive scene caused by environmental developments and political tremors. Your strengths may be in your material resources, your special knowledge, power of communication, contact building skills or an analytical bend of mind. Your weaknesses may be embedded in your inability to rise above the detail to see the bigger picture, procrastination or your mercurial temperament. In the age of information the more you know about your own self and the situation you are in, the better will be your decision making and brighter the prospects of your success.

Corporates need competitive intelligence to draw up an effective business strategy precisely because out there in the market you cannot have your way merely on your own strength. The outcome of your business plan may be determined by the intervention of a smaller but smarter competitor of whom you did not have any idea. Information of intelligence value is required for due diligence, vender verification, political assessments, evaluation of geo-location risks and the moves of the other players in the market. Many strategic decisions in the corporate world are incremental in nature based on the logic dictated by what has been happening in the present and what had happened in the past. When something unforeseen happens like a new player arriving on the scene with better decision-making tools and better alignment of its work force to the business goals, this logic breaks and the older corporation suffers on account of intelligence failure.

Being intelligent means being updated not only about your own set up but also being well-informed about your competition. Once you decide what you want to know, the where? and the how? for accessing it can be rationally pursued. The competitors will be doing hiring, procurement, banking, advertising and data processing. Each of these activities will involve interaction with the world outside - the service agencies, contract workers and consultants giving you enough openings for legitimate collection of information. Intelligent organizations create their own information gathering systems.

It is necessary to study the profile of the strengths as well as the weak spots of the other players on your turf, both old and new. In today's highly interactive and interdependent world there is no escape from your having to understand the human, sociological and business situation around you. You have to keenly evaluate your own strengths and weaknesses, of course. Buying a company at an opportune time, acquiring a new technology from a startup in the field and introducing a new product that offers an extra promise, are the moves that an intelligent player makes to add to his strength. At the same time he is vigilant against the prying attempts of the competitor to get to his proprietary technology or protected information and to seduce his key personnel. Even when you are in the lead the challenge of change will still test your ability to retain the edge.

If you know your strengths and weaknesses as an entrepreneur you can seek out such people for your team who can make up for you in the areas where you need complementarity. This calls for some shedding of ego on your part so that you would be willing later to acknowledge the contribution of those who came on board. Infosys is a good example of an enterprise working on its strength, the software development and consciously keeping away from the challenge of diversification of business after having tested waters on the manufacture side once.

The laws of evolution apply to businesses inasmuch as the latter are an extension of human activity. An enterprise has to be smart and not merely 'strong' in terms of the muscle power of liquidity or brand image. Dinosaurs perished only because they failed in the area of brain-power. Being smart is a corollary of being intelligent. An intelligent person does not allow greed to become his primary motive for becoming rich. Greed can push you on the wrong side of law and morality. Some of the biggest leaders of business have been, in recent times, hauled up before the courts of criminal justice because they were gripped by this weakness and did things that were dumb. It is unintelligent not to do anything about such of your traits as make you weak or about matters that ultimately mar the brand value of your business. Businesses under competition are compelled to walk the evolutionary track. Those who have strength of leadership will have the generic advantage in the scenario of 'the survival of the fittest' that is overtaking the world of business.

Another facet of all business being a part of the human domain is the great sensitivity that it shows to political environ which itself is set by the society. Any political development that induces instability hits the business scene hard because politics represents the larger human matrix of which business activity is a part. This underscores the importance of intelligence for business. Political analysis is a major input for assessing the competitive environ that contains seeds of vulnerabilities as also the promise of opportunities for business.

In competitive business the survival of the fittest may induce companies to build joint ventures with the objective of monopolizing the market and pushing weaker players aside. Already in a global scenario the strong entities are also becoming smarter in terms of enhancing customer loyalty by investing more in quality control and showing resilience on pricing just to score over the rivals. Buy-outs and forced takeovers of smaller players is a part of this phenomenon. Pareto's law – 'a few govern the many' is beginning to apply to the market place just as it has always operated on the political front where the elites managed to rule the masses. Globalization and its evolutionary offspring, the competition, was likely to set a trend of the rise of what can be construed as economic imperialism. An intelligent entity will be able to survive and progress in this interplay of strength and weakness.

The key is to realize that the success of a few will not make sense if it means the defeat of all others. This holds good in politics as well as in economics as both benefit only so long as resentment and revolution do not cause instability. Being intelligent means achieving victory without making enemies. This is perhaps why Corporate Social Responsibility is emerging as a strategic objective for firms who wish to succeed in the long range.

Globalization, because of the built-in safe guard of competition, will hopefully not become an instrument for the return of exploitative capitalism. Those who are in the business of making profits have to be intelligent enough to avoid becoming a victim of their own strengths and overreach. The great financial meltdown sparked off in the US in the middle of 2008 could be traced, among other things, to the reckless desire for profits verging on greed on the part of Lehman Brothers, the largest mortgage bank of America. One consequence of this downturn is that risk-management, until recently an unpopular elective, is expected to become an important part of many B Schools' curricula in the coming years.

Business environment is affected by the mix of culture, commerce and technology and it is necessary to scan it constantly for change vectors. For the foresight function to operate on a note of success, it has to have the benefit of a disciplined process in place to spot new patterns and potential changes and bring these to the notice of the organisation's leadership for prompt action. Open sources of intelligence provide an important channel for monitoring the environment. However, to get an idea of what the competitors are upto, skills of gathering intelligence may have to be pressed into use because the latter would have kept their cards close to their chest.

Everybody needs to deal with change and try to stay ahead of the curve even in the face of ambiguity. To be able to process the complexity of a situation and form a view of patterns that are just emerging, is basic to achieving progress in today's world. Noting and analyzing the external landscape is the new call for entrepreneurs. In the post-cold war era globalization has altered the supply and demand scene of the world because of the sudden rise of new economies. The strategic environ has generally been transforming so fast that macro-economic trends have overtaken the business world by surprise[5]. A positive feature, however, is that opportunities have also multiplied for any player who is determined to go for them ahead of others. It is not enough to lean on experts for advice about the future. You have to be your own observer and analyst as for as the broad spectrum of externalities is concerned. For this you have to be well informed about the competitive environ and also be aware of the connectivity of facts that would be there when knowledge begins unfolding as part of an integral packaging, relevant to your area of business or profession. The evolution of knowledge throws up new information but tracking its connectivities will help you foresee the direction of what lies ahead provided both observation and analysis is sharp.

To be able to form a forward-looking view of the outside world is a measure of being intelligent. Every business today operates in a complex societal and political milieu that demands more of attention on fronts other than just profits. There are issues to be tackled that go beyond the market. They may range from illegal immigration to stem cell research. Their impact is enlarged by the special interest groups who have acquired a new-found importance. Internet has given such groups an unprecedented access and an ability to disseminate views at low cost that can cause seismic changes in the world of business by affecting the acceptance of products.

The political process often has a significant impact on business and it is essential that one understood the ramifications of legislation and regulations for one's business and industry. Some shifts in the political scene are transformational and intelligence lies in evaluating if they pose a threat or bring in an opportunity. Detection of breaks in the continuity of the external landscape, if supplemented by imagination, can help you anticipate the shape of things to come and reposition the business for further advancement.

Your strength lies in being able to change things that are under your control. Outside of that control are a host of external factors including other people's responses and decisions. You are working on your strengths and therefore you should invest your energy only on what you have influence on and not waste it on things that are not under your control. Step out of your comfort zone, do not get stuck with the status quo and try to push through without fear when invoking your strengths. It is a sign of inner strength to accept that you are primarily responsible for what you achieve or do not achieve. Do not blame others for your misfortune or setback. This is a weakness to be avoided. You should accept the ownership of your destiny, this will get you in the habit of marshalling your strengths.

Endnotes

1. *Times of India,* Dec. 30, 2007, '*The Promise of the Personal Genome*'.
2. *Go Put Your Strengths to Work,* Marcus Beechingham, Simon & Schuster, London, 2007
3. *Hindustan Times,* Delhi Feb. 5, 2008.
4. *Hindustan Times,* Delhi, Feb 5, 2008.
5. '*Know How*', Ram Charan Crown Business, New York, 2007

11 Understanding Confidentiality

In the entire animal kingdom, it is the human mind alone that is gifted by nature with the ability to keep one's thoughts locked up inside and bring them out only at will. This is a powerful instrument of control that you have with you while dealing with others. Confidentiality gives you the wherewithal to access and preserve knowledge that you legitimately wish to use exclusively for your own good. Sometimes you keep your perceptions to yourself as you either do not want to be impolite to the other person during an interaction or wish to use what you have noted, at some other point of time later. Confidentiality helps you handle your responsibilities more effectively on the basis of the feedback that you manage to get on your work environ through undisclosed channels. You can come closer to your boss if you are the type he can share his views with, in confidence.

Confidential information is at par with intelligence and it must, if it is going to be put to use, satisfy the two vital tests of reliability and utility that characterize the latter. Credibility of the source or channel from where the information has come to you must be established. It is important that you do not lap up misinformation that someone motivated by a personal agenda has dished out to you. Even when the source of your information is trustworthy the facts should be evaluated before being accepted. As regards utility it should be understood that confidentiality is an aid to decision-making. Once the information has played itself out in the sense that open action on it has been completed, it loses the tag of confidentiality. Confidentiality is an instrument that comes in handy in strengthening your response to an event or development. It is also practised when a reason exists, personal or organizational, that calls for non-disclosure. Incidentally confidentiality does not apply to information that you may be legally obliged to disclose. It is a personal privilege that you enjoy without intending to cause any harm to the society.

The information that you have gained confidentially may not be something that pleases you but this cannot be the reason enough for discarding it. Being intelligent means having a developed capacity to make use of both positive and negative feedback[1]. Use confidentiality to plan for dealing with the demon outside and also to reform yourself from within by eliminating the flaws that you have been made aware of. Confidentiality enables you to do good and combat the evil.

Being intelligent means being rational and the ability to keep a secret connects with the rational evaluation of what needs to be kept confidential. Is the scientific research that believes mind reading is possible likely to adversely impact on this ability? Dr. Jack Gallant of the University of California at Berkeley says: 'it may be possible to reconstruct the picture of a person's visual experience from measurement of brain activity alone[2]. The technique being experienced with is called Functional Magnetic

Resource Imaging (FMRI) that creates images of brain activity based on changes in blood flow to different brain regions and makes it possible to observe patterns of such activity when a person examined was exposed to a range of visuals. While it is true that mind-reading machines, if invented, would change the way we live in, the FMRI experimentation would at best only give an idea of how an object or scene is being perceived by an observer in terms of its emotional impact. The application of intelligence in analysis, evaluation and decision-making will remain an individual's personal domain. The determination of what should be kept confidential will very much be a part of this domain. The FMRI may possibly become a component of forensic science but keeping things confidential will remain an integral part of personal freedom.

Understanding confidentiality and keeping a particular knowledge to yourself requires a certain amount of mental strength. *Svetasvatara Upanishad* says: 'hold the reins of your mind as you would hold the reins of a restive horse'. Confidentiality does not go well with weak-minded individuals. It is a positive trait, a competence that the team leader likes to see in the members working with him on a mission that requires averting premature disclosure of the strategy, for its success. Being intelligent means being cognizant of the fact that sometimes one gets the best results from information by keeping it under the wrap till it was put to its best use.

A smart business enterprise is not only information savvy but is also fully aware of the value of confidentiality in dealing with the competitive environment. The merit of being transparent and upfront in dealing with your customers is one thing and the necessity of protecting your trade secrets is quite another. We live in a world where there are lurking forces out to misuse somebody else's private domain and make an intrusive peep into somebody's proprietary information. The adversary has in its armoury a number of instruments and techniques that can be used by him to penetrate into the protected sphere of your firm's activity. The awareness about this can be fostered through security orientation programmes conducted as part of human resource development. Identity theft, already the number one crime in US and rapidly expanding throughout the Internet world, was expected to increase at a faster pace in the coming years and this could wreck havoc on the financial and social lives of millions around the globe. Being intelligent means being cognizant of the security situation in which one operates. A firm is not impeded by the threats from the rivals per se; it becomes vulnerable only when it fails to understand them and take adequate safeguards against them. If you can keep it confidentially to yourself that you have an idea of what the other side had planned, the advantage is all yours.

A well informed leader or entrepreneur has to know that today new threats are overtaking the conventional security risks that nations and businesses faced earlier. The world is engaged in low intensity cyber conflicts characterized by aggressive enemy efforts to collect intelligence on the target country's weapons, power grids and even financial markets. In 2007, US reported 44,000 incidents of malicious cyber activity, one third more than the previous year and more than ten times as many as in 2001.[3] In 2007-08, Russia blocked all the websites of Estonia and Georgia by perpetrating 'denial of service' attacks. A serious danger on the horizon is the threat of sabotage that the information systems face from the counterfeit chips being produced on a large scale. In

January 2008 the FBI reported that 3600 counterfeit CISCO network components were discovered inside US defence and power systems.[4] The new threat pertains to the hardware rather than the familiar field of software. Being intelligent means being continually well informed about developments that had a bearing on your avocation or business and the security situation around it.

At work and at home confidentiality and privacy are the instruments that an intelligent person wields to his advantage. If you know something about your adversary or the competitor, without the latter being aware of this, the knowledge you have becomes a source of power for you so long as you handle it confidentially. Intelligent persons know what should be said or treated in confidence even when they are being upfront and open-hearted in dealing with others. In the world we live in today, there are elements out there who were engaged whole time in accessing personal information of others and having an intrusive peep into their domain of privacy for evil intentions. Ability to use the legitimacy of confidentiality comes from a developed sense of discretion which is a trait associated with intelligent people.

Confidentiality does not have the negativity of an act of hiding, much less of telling a lie or misdirecting somebody else. It is in fact a measure of responsibility and commitment towards a positive objective that its possessor is trying to achieve. Confidentiality is not meant to cause harm to anybody even as it serves the cause of the individual and his organization. Intelligent people know that premature disclosures can mar the prospects of reaching out to their goal. Large heavily worked enterprises do have a certain transparency about the organization's mission and working but they also follow the 'need to know' principle internally as this enhances both security and productivity. Intelligent leadership ensures that no one is needlessly burdened with information that does not relate to his role in the organization. This helps the members to give their total attention and energy to the task at hand. It is also necessary to understand that the meaning of the word 'friendship' should not be misconstrued to compel total sharing of all personal and professional information within one's circle. Being intelligent means being respectful towards the other person's right to maintain an area of confidentiality in regard to matters that do not concern you.

Confidentiality is often interpreted as a licence to keep information from others within the organization. Even the meaning of restrictive security is apparently not fully understood. The 'need to know' principle on which this rests does not apply to those who are vertically above you in the hierarchy. It is basically designed to check unauthorized spread of sensitive information horizontally and downwards. The higher you are in the hierarchy the greater is your accountability about not permitting confidential information to be breached. Reluctance to share information for misplaced reasons of feeling powerful or scoring over colleagues is not what confidentiality is all about. In many companies even the senior people may not know what is happening in different wings of their enterprise. Confidentiality is important in the context of inner meetings and discussions where internal weaknesses may be brought to the table. Anything breathing out may damage the company's fortune and competitive strength. Appropriate confidentiality both internally and externally is therefore important for any enterprise. Lack of it may signify low morale or disenchantment among the employees. Also, if somebody is credulous or given to falling for gossip he will also not be good at keeping things confidential. In an organization that puts premium on self-discipline, members also have a better understanding of confidentiality.

Endnotes

1. *'What got you here, Won't get you there'*. Marshall Gold Smith, Hyperion, New York, 2007
2. *Hindustan Times,* March 7, 2008.
3. *Securing the Information Highway,* Wesley K. Clark and Peter Levin, *Foreign Affairs,* Nov- Dec 2009
4. *Foreign Affairs,* Nov- Dec 2009

12 Awareness and Acceptance

Knowledge is the true path to real detachment. Being intelligent means being aware of what has to be accepted and being able to get the maximum returns for what you have, in terms of satisfaction and peace that comes with it. We are so wrapped up in the thoughts of what we seek that we do not enjoy what we already have. Awareness when combined with acceptance opens the gateway to bliss. If you have the awareness of the positives and negatives in your situation and willingness to accept the outcome of the best effort that you could make in that situation, this itself will set you apart as a human being of exceptional quality. If you have been a person who did not willfully harm others and who kept endeavoring to reach a goal with faith in your own self, you are entitled to make a celebration of this basic success.

Awareness and acceptance put you on a grid where your inputs have maximum energy and where the output is greeted with equanimity. The earlier you can reach this grid in your life the more rewarding will be the time that lies ahead of you. Operating on this grid intelligent people are able to make choices that best suit their temperament for competition, their work-life balance and their value system. It is the awareness that helps you to mature with experience. Awareness is a function of mind while aging is an aspect of the body. An aware mind grows even when there is aging of the body. Such a mind interprets the journey of life on a note of understanding and freedom from the greatest of fears – the fear of death.

It is awareness that facilitates acceptance and makes way for a life of greater fulfillment. 'If predictability is about what will happen and when, understanding is about why and how'.[1] Ever so often in our lives we can benefit from this in exercising our options. A woman in a career has to decide how important is her urge for motherhood with the awareness that this could, in her case, possibly slow down her progress on the professional ladder. Quest for an office of public responsibility could require sacrificing some privacy and mental peace. Commitment to social service or fulfillment of the desire to be close to nature could be behind somebody choosing not to become part of a corporate bureaucracy functioning from a dense metropolis. Some people opt for early retirement. Some others give up plum salaries to launch their own entrepreneurship. It is the convergence of awareness and acceptance that often lies behind your best decisions. The powerful combination of awareness and acceptance keeps you to the path of stability, tranquility and maximalism. Awareness comes from knowledge, from the realization that what is positive or negative is also relative and from the thought that there is a larger picture of life in which whatever is happening, has to be seen. Acceptance provides contentment, resilience and moral strength against odds.

Awareness is linked to the ability to see things from a higher perspective. To get a bird's eye view literally of 'the scene below' is to realize how in proximity every object and issue looks big but when you see things from above it finds its relatively small slot in the wider scheme. Only from an airplane can you see the big reality of earth being round. Caught between the micro and the macro, the small and the large, human beings are handicapped by a life attuned to the middle space. 'We are not equipped to perceive atoms and germs on one end of the scale or galaxies and expanding universes on the other'[2]. We are likely to pay attention to and remember short-term trends and small number runs. The few decades of a human lifetime is far too short to witness evolution, continental drift or long-term environmental changes. Intelligent people, however, accept the validation of what lies in the long range.

There is growing awareness in the corporate world that in a situation where success is measured by who can log the most hours, it was necessary for the personnel to be saved from getting burnt out. According to the Society of Human Resources the percentage of large companies in the US offering Sabbaticals to their managers has steadily increased in recent years. Paid or partially paid leave from work is proving an effective means of recharging the human resource and strengthening the element of corporate loyalty as an additional advantage.

Work and fun, however, need not become antithetical to each other. If you enjoy doing what you do you can be a healthy 'workaholic'. If you are interested in the work assigned to you, you will be able to remain focused on it more easily which in turn will enhance your efficacy, productivity and the level of performance. Your work-life balance then is also positively impacted because you do not carry that much of burden home. As the distractions caused by the workplace are minimized, the quality of personal time spent by you on your own self will also improve. Being intelligent means having fun in whatever you are engaged in – be it working, exercising or just interacting with others. My days at the University were easily among the most enjoyable periods of my life simply because study was fun, never a slog.

Intelligent people are aware of the importance of work-life balance and they attend to the priorities not only at work but also at home[3]. They do not expect their employers to sort this out for them. Remember, if you are so busy with work that you find no time to eat, you may psychologically start liking being in this situation, as you believe it props up your image as a person of commitment. You should be wary of missing a meal to fit work. This may lead you to the habit of working even on weekends to achieve perfection in disregard of health and the larger well-being. Some such people develop the psychosis that if they took a vacation they might miss out on something important happening in their absence.

To strive for a goal and relish making the effort for it is what is important. The wisdom to accept what comes at the end of it comes from an awareness of the larger meaning of a purposeful life. Life is a journey and the travel must be enjoyed even when it is tedious in parts because here the 'goal' is also the 'end'. Being intelligent means identifying the right set of objectives and then being on the quest for achieving them. You should feel the joy of active pursuit keeping the focus on your progress and not on the comparison of your situation with somebody else's. Success is life in reflected in the self-esteem that comes to you when you complete a mission. Your win need not be somebody else's defeat. Awareness helps you to be bold when you lose and calm when you win.

Winston Churchill said 'success is not final, failure is not fatal: it is the courage to continue that counts'.

Awareness of the larger scene of life makes the acceptance of all the hassles of the immediate, easy. St. Francis of Assisi makes a point about our ability to differentiate between what is in our control and what is not in these words: 'God grant me the serenity to accept the things I cannot change, courage to change the things I can; and wisdom to know the difference'. Resilience is acquired through self-awareness. It is the exposure to a range of difficult circumstances and the effort to overcome them that helps build it up. It is with resilience that you ride out a crisis or danger. Resilience also helps to banish extreme anxiety that obstructs clear thinking in an emergency and damages your capacity to imagine what lies ahead that called for action. As Madame Curie said: 'nothing in life is to be feared, it is only to be understood'.

Awareness is a stress buster. It reduces the impact of negative thoughts that clog your mind. It sets the ground for making an objective interpretation of any event or experience and thus facilitates the process by which you can move on. It is awareness that would stand guard at the door of your mind and enable you to consciously dissociate from responses of hatred, anger or jealousy. Awareness keeps you in the ambit of positive thoughts from where you are more likely to initiate positive action and succeed. Awareness acts as a corrective when belief systems sometimes cloud the vision and mar free-thinking. Awareness that every action is an experience even if it does not lead to the desired outcome, reduces the adverse impact of 'failure' as it is commonly understood.

Life is a finite time given to you by nature, to be put to its best use. No two lives have an identical graph of highs and lows. Your life is an experience that is yours alone. It is your exclusive story and this makes you a special person. You have your own moments of joy and setback. Your sense of regret and deprivation, if not rooted in your own willful acts, almost always arises from a needless comparison with the others' lot. The choices you made and the results they brought should be accepted in a spirit of celebrating life.

An aspect of awareness is the realization that our own view of things might be founded on particular geo-political, ethnic, ideological, domestic or professional perspectives and that there could always be an equally valid 'other view' coming from somewhere else. As someone said 'it is going to be necessary for us to leave home in order to find it'[4]. In a globalized world this realization comes easily to those who are well informed and whose intelligence is blended with the right kind of emotional and spiritual quotient. Moreover, awareness is what can help today's managers to meet the difficult requirement of balancing local demands with a global vision. In fact this balancing is the best test of awareness that a globalized existence demands of any successful person. Awareness gives you a wider view that in turn provides the correct parameters for the decision that you may take in relation to any event, development or scenario confronted locally.

Among the finer points of awareness is the realization that there is nothing absolute about the course that your life will take. Being secure is predictably considered to be the prime objective of life. Retention of health, acquisition of wealth and a guarantee of protection against attacks from hostile quarters, constitute the powerful mix that makes for the ultimate perceptions of security. Intelligent people, however, realize that these sources of security themselves are vulnerable to shifts. They know that security is a matter of degree. The complex dynamics of life at best create simulated stability. Being intelligent means that you do not take security for granted and remain prepared for changes that might affect your personal resourcefulness or alter the profile of environment that envelops you.

Some of the greatest thinking people acknowledge the Indian thought that calls for an awareness of what is mortal and what is everlasting. Ralph Waldo Emerson, the philosopher described *Bhagwad Gita* as 'the voice of an old intelligence which in another age and climate had pondered and thus disposed of the same questions which exercise us'. Another philosopher Arthur Schopenhauer said of the study of *Upnishads:* 'it has been the solace of my life, it will be the solace of my death'. Albert Einstein was impacted by the time and space phenomenon described by *Bhagwad Gita* in 'God's own words' as he put it. Einstein said: 'when I read *Bhagwad Gita* and reflect about how God created this Universe everything else seems so superfluous'. These great thinkers were pushing further the frontiers of awareness by traversing the dividing line between science and philosophy. They were in fact underscoring the importance of imagination as the enhancer of knowledge.

It is rare to find a person who would not, given another chance, like to relive at least parts of his life differently. Success in life can be measured by the satisfaction one has when, looking back at any point in the journey of life, one finds that not many moments were wasted on faulty pursuits or purposeless existence. Intelligent people are attuned to deriving quick lessons from their own experiences as also from the lives of others. They also guard against developing a victim's mentality. You should not let a setback push you into a persecution complex or a misfortune mania. It is common to find people succumbing to a sense of total loss just because there is an intemperate spouse at home, a negative boss at work place or a business that has shown signs of decline.

Being intelligent means making an early analysis of where you stand on the awareness-acceptance paradigm and decide what options you have for further action. Find out what you can do to avoid running into a lasting negativity. Is there a need for you to do an introspection to determine how you can improve upon your own role and performance? Your awareness will help you to decide in what way you should accept the situation and continue or plan to quit and relocate. Intelligent people are capable of being self-reflective. This sharpens their awareness of their own responses as also of their place in the scheme of things. To be able to see our own role in whatever happens and accept the outcome accordingly is the hallmark of intelligence.

There is a positive side to every experience even if it was otherwise a painful one. Any transition through a crisis is an opportunity for reinvention of some kind. People who have a developed sense of awareness are able to see the upside in any situation.

Acceptance would be meaningful only if awareness is complete. Awareness is not only the observation and understanding of all the externalities that you encounter but a conscious notice too of your own thought processes and subjectivity. You should not only observe and discreetly absorb the scene around but also scrutinize if your intended responses are rational. If you can trace the roots of your emotions, obsessions and motivations, you would be in command of your situation and get the best results out of your endeavour. It all boils down to the recipe of being able to act as the witness to your own thinking and action. This is the ultimate awareness and a powerful multiplier of performance. Being aware is inseparable from being intelligent.

Mark Twain said: 'twenty years from now you will be more disappointed by the things that you did not do than by the ones you did do'. So live a little. Fun is a vital ingredient of quality life. You should have interests outside of your work. This might ultimately help you to feel less guilty about what you did not do. Pursuit of excellence is desirable but it should not become a craze for being perfect in everything, big or small. Note that this suggests an inability to distinguish between what is significant and what is critically important. This can disturb the correlation between time and effort without your even realizing it.

Endnotes

1. *How to be a good boss in a bad economy,* Robert I. Sutton, *Harvard Business Review,* June 2009.
2. *Folk Numeracy and Middle Land,* Michael Shermer, *Scientific American,* September 2008.
3. *Winning,* Jack Welch, Harper Collins, 2005.
4. *New Directions in Creative and Innovative Management,* Vol. 7, edited by Yuji Ijiri, Robert Lawrance Kuhn, 1988, Ballinger Publishing Company Cambridge, Massachusetts.

13 Time is a Resource

The transition of the world to the 'age of knowledge', thanks to the IT revolution, has given a new, found importance to the speed with which business is transacted today. It has made this a determinant of competitive advantage. 'We have made a Bing Bang with the Web and everything is cooling and solidifying at a ferocious pace'[1].The gap between information and decision and that between a considered decision and action has to be minimized. The upshot of this is that we have to have the realization of time being a precious resource, an asset that is not renewable. Being intelligent means getting attuned to the value of time and ensuring that, both at work place as well as at home, time is not wasted. Time is a commodity that is not to be squandered away. Being seemingly busy is not the same thing as being productive. Even leisure is to be distinguished from mere idling away of time. Moreover, while everyone should strive to improve upon time-management, it should be clearly understood that averting a waste of time and doing things in haste are two different things.

An Intelligence organization that is devoted to safeguarding national security is trained for doing its job without any avoidable loss of time. It works for speedy collection of information, its quick analysis and an instant reporting. The organization's management is designed to make sure that execution of operations is not impeded by bureaucratic 'structure' or a delayed communication. Its management practices are geared to achieving quick results and some of them may be worthy of emulation by institutions that run senior management training programmes.[2] When I was the chief of Intelligence Bureau I regarded 15 minutes as a workable unit of time for review meetings, interactions with visitors and clearing an operational project.

If time is a resource, its consumption should be accurately estimated. No business plan can guarantee success unless it knows how much can be achieved in a time-frame and works out a schedule for measuring the output of an employee on a day-to-day basis. A key to productivity is to establish a healthy pressure of work as this normally helps minimize the waste of time. Having the right information in time, reaching a knowledge based decision with speed and quickly communicating the details of the plan to all those who are concerned with execution, these together constitute an integral package that is adopted by an intelligent organization in pursuit of success. Even the top management of a firm may not be information savvy to the point of knowing when should the accumulated and collated data be considered adequate for decision-making and when should the action on that decision be launched. Importance of communication of the plan to those who were to work on it, cannot be overemphasized. The skills of conveying the agenda in simple, unambiguous and concise terms remain in short supply. The leadership of an intelligent organization must, therefore, ensure that communication lines up and down the hierarchy are flawless, easy and free of hassles.

Accessing and handling information and maintaining a smooth communication system within the organization are emerging as new lines of consultancy business. All this is a dimension of the new realization that a maximal utilization of time as a resource is a prime requisite for gaining a competitive edge. It is the significance of time as a resource that has created new thinking on how to remain focused on the work at hand, how to consciously get rid of the habit of procrastination and how to add value to a process by eliminating avoidable waste of moments. Benjamin Franklin, one of the founding fathers of the US, rightly said: 'time is money'. It is interesting how the idea that time is a precious resource is changing our socio-economic life. Part-time employments, product development aimed at meeting the user's preference for easy consumption and value creation through a compressed assembly line movement, are some of the manifestations of the importance of time as a resource. Sharing the ownership of a resort on the basis of divided time, for usage, is an emerging business.

Leadership today is largely about the ability to get more from a team in less time. The rise of an entire industry based on technology that provides time tracking tools is yet another evidence of the value of time as a resource, in fact a resource that is scarce for the simple reason that it cannot be replenished. Intelligent people manage to identify and eliminate time stealers in any situation and try to use their time more effectively. Parents would do well to supplement the effort of the teachers to inculcate the awareness of the importance of time amongst the students. Discipline, in a major sense, is rooted in this awareness.

Awareness of the value of time as a precious resource calls for an acceptance of the need to prioritize the tasks that you must take up first at any given time. Your capacity for distinguishing essentials from non-essentials, your vision that draws a line between what is of immediate importance and what would be required in the long run and your intrinsic ability to concentrate on whatever you do, all these put you on the top of any performance chart. Prioritization should not result in the neglect of the 'routine', should not destroy the work-life balance and should not detract from your willingness to carry out the task that your team leader has given you.

Ready access to useful information comes at a cost, both of money and time. Seekers of information must bear in mind the fact that with the increase in the volume of information the line between what is worthwhile and what is unimportant and a mere distraction, tends to wear thin. Technological aids do help to manage information but ultimately the threat of information overload that can clearly kill productivity, has to be tackled by the information seeker only by developing a mind-set that effortlessly picks up only those facts that are relevant to the larger objective at hand. Being intelligent means having a clear understanding of the inverse relationship between time as a precious resource and acquisition of information that helps decision making. One should know when to stop collecting information and see if a decision can be taken on the available knowledge to initiate action. Some people remain endlessly in the phase of accessing information because they lose sight of the value of time as a resource. Remember, knowledge is useful if it helps to guide you into the future.

Loss of time occurs more commonly between the moment when decision has been taken and the point where implementation of the plan commences. It is largely because, for a variety of reasons, the communication of the plan details to the concerned quarters responsible for action consumes time. In the context of national security, failures have occurred more for lack of action due to delayed communication than for the reason of inadequacy of information. Imperfect communications resulting in misinterpretations, bureaucratic impediments in the smooth two-way communication across the vertical hierarchy and sheer lethargy on the part of those accountable for execution, are the frequent causes that result in critical loss of time culminating in project failure. The remedy lies in a robust training for developing a mind-set that values time as a resource.

Such a mind-set enhances the understanding of the importance of doing things on a note of urgency even when nobody is watching. It reinforces the capacity to concentrate on the task at hand. In an enterprise it is loyalty and the sense of commitment that becomes a determinant of how devoted the work force would be to the implementation of the plan. There should be an unceasing effort to bring about constant improvement and one way of doing this is to ensure that wastage of time is eliminated. Japanese automobile industries are said to have added to the quality and cost effectiveness by placing suppliers in the close proximity of manufactures that contributed to inventory control. This is an illustration of how considering time as a precious resource increases productivity. An efficient organization stands on this understanding.

The optimal use of time as a resource is facilitated by skillful time management, increased concentration on the work at hand that would minimize waste of moments and a discreet sequencing of priorities to get the best results for the long term. Our time management skills are tested by the success with which we can handle multi-tasking. Developing the habit of doing any work with a sense of urgency enhances the power of concentration. The ability to judge the relative importance of a task in a given context or under an accepted strategy is rare and it comes from the innate sense of viewing essentials differently from the non-essentials in the given scheme of things. Time management, like any other sphere of management, calls for a planned approach to work. Objective, means available and a mechanism to monitor progress are the three facets of a task that would need to be defined if they have to be the part of an action plan. Trying to do the same work in less time or producing more in the same time without telling on the quality of production, is something that is relatable to your belief in the goal, your optimism about your success in achieving it and your stakes in doing it in quick time. Together this all will create that sense of urgency which enhances the power of concentration. Finally, if time is a resource, your timing about the work at hand should be sound too. Being intelligent means being able to get this timing right on the strength of an appreciation of what is relatively more significant in a given moment or context. Time saved from being spent on non-essentials will be a resource added for investment on fruitful ventures.

Endnotes

1. *Content Critical,* Gerry Mc Govern, *Financial Times,* Prentice Hall, October, 2001
2. *Intelligence – A Security Weapon,* DC Pathak, Manas Publications, Delhi, 2004

14 Man above Technology

Technology, a product of innovativeness of the human mind, always sub serves the objectives that man sets for himself. It is an extension of intelligence in the sense that it provides man with an added outreach to the information that he wants to access. It is a facilitator or an aid for unraveling knowledge. The interpretation of what it reveals, however, lies in the human domain. Technology helps in deciphering an opportunity or identifying a threat and acts as an instrument for executing a course of action. It is however, ultimately only a weapon in the hands of man. Man is the master of technology; it can never be the other way round. Being intelligent means being clear about the fundamental relationship between S&T and man.

One can run into serious pitfalls if this is not understood. The IT revolution has transformed the system of communication in terms of the speed of transmission and the expanse of information that can be reached on the internet. However, it would be unintelligent, for instance, to presume that the facts and data on the net are always reliable. The findings posted by Think Tanks or Business analysis syndicates on the net, likewise, cannot be accepted blindly as the gospel truth. The sane advice here is that you accept the facts if they are validated but do not necessarily, borrow the findings. You must reserve the right to establish the credibility of the facts before accepting them. Technology does produce authentic data whose evaluation will always rest in human hands. Technology has, no doubt, universally helped the data processing exercise but remember that all statistical indicators for analysis are set by man himself. Data processing enables human beings to examine and utilize formidable amount of facts or information for making analytical assessments. Technology, however, cannot substitute for human imagination and forward thinking that is required for anticipating on the basis of available information, what lies ahead in the invisible future. Technology can create 'information overload' but it can also help alleviate it which again highlights the fact of its being a neutral instrument. All software products are the enabling tools for processing and diagnostic functions. They are travel aids not the destinations. Technology is a means not an end product.

Technology impacted development and growth on one hand and instigated a revolution in military affairs, on the other. Andrew Marshall of the office of the US Secretary of State has defined RMA as 'a major change in the nature of warfare brought about by the innovative application of new technologies which, combined with dramatic changes in military doctrine, operational and organizational concepts, fundamentally alters the character and conduct of military operations'. However, even when war is completely permeated by technology and even governed by it, the decisions about its objectives and directions will always be in the hands of men.

The year 2007 established a milestone in the march of man towards the era of cyber warfare. The emerging threat from cyber attackers was the apparent reason why the US

Air Force quietly decided to form a Cyber Space Command. Just 20 years after the start of the internet there is prospect of a warfare being unleashed online. The attack on information systems on which the conduct of strategic and military responses is vitally anchored, represents a new theater of combat. The age of information ushered in by the IT revolution has not only globalized the economy but has also made all strategic activity dependent on highly protected information systems. An attack on these systems by way of hacking and data destruction can make fortified positions vulnerable. Cyber warfare has emerged as a new determinant of the kind of offensive an adversary can launch. In China the PLA is said to be researching an e-bomb as an answer to the threat posed to it by the Nuclear Missile Defence (NMD) of the USA. In the wake of 9/11 safe storage of backup electronic data has acquired a new found importance worldwide. Being intelligent today means being aware of the impact of technology on the society at large.

Technology innovation has enabled the Americans to induct robots into their fighting force. In mid - 2007 the US Army deployed the first armed robots in Iraq marking a new era in modern warfare. The new 'special weapons observation remote reconnaissance direct action system' (SWORDS) can open fire on a target from more than 3000 feet away[1]. A few of these robots each costing $ 250,000, have been tried in Iraq in the dangerous ground zones to reduce the risk on soldier's lives. The use of Drones, the unmanned airplanes by the US troops for bombing the terrorist hideouts on the Pak-Afghan border, is the recent contribution of technology to the modern combat. Technology is now the new trend-setter in an asymmetric warfare in which one side is resorting to the use of 'human bombs' to take on an opponent who had a much superior arsenal at his command.

Technology is the extended arm of man. In the area of security it substitutes for human entity in surveillance operations, facilitates listening without being in the proximity of the target and makes intrusion detection possible even when you are not there to protect your private space or territory. It is used for both offence and defence particularly when the enemy is engaged in making covert attacks. More extensive, however, is the use of technology outside of the sphere of warfare. It brings in new products and facilities the cause of service of humanity. It has globalized human thinking by making it possible for people to stay connected in real time regardless of distances. It has helped man to dig into the 'secrets' of nature to discover new medicines, mineral resources and productivity enhancers. It has added to the efficiency and cost effectiveness of all human operations. It has sharpened and strengthened the will-power of man. It has prompted socio-cultural revolutions. And finally, as already mentioned, it has altered the military techniques and thinking. In all this what it would never be able to do is to subordinate or enslave the mind of man to its own self. Robots will always be under the command of man not the vice versa.

Technology is impacting on social customs and culture by offering acceptable and convenient options to rituals that could sometimes be performed with the help of the internet. There are cases where young married women who are working or whose husbands have a job in a different location and for that reason not being in a position to spend the evening of a traditional Hindu festival like *Karva Chauth* with the wife, are reported to have completed the ceremony using the 'virtual' medium. The husband's face could be seen on the webcam screen before breaking the fast and even live interaction could be had using video-conference technique. All this illustrates the way social attitudes and thinking are influenced by technology options that do not, at the same time, create any 'culture deficit' for the family.

Technological advancement has boosted business enterprises by helping to create new products and services. All business is a human endeavour and man has got technology to serve his objectives in his personal and professional spheres. Gillette achieved leadership in shaving business because of its research and development capabilities that used 270 researchers, 160 of whom had PhDs in chemistry, metallurgy, physics, mathematics and engineering to look into every aspect of the science and art of shaving. Mach3 cartridges, with three blades of imported stainless steel stropped to an edge fifty times sharper than a surgical scalpel, were assembled with nine other parts into a plastic cartridge at the rate of 600 units per minute.[2] The allowable defect tolerance was zero and this was made possible by use of robotics. The Gillette technology was produced by man and put into the service of the business enterprise.

Exponential growth in computational power made it possible for the human genome project to be completed within the scheduled 15 years. Seven years in, the genome was only 1% sequenced but doublings in processing power had the project finished on schedule. However, we are nowhere near seriously contending that computational power one day can close the gap between machine and human intelligence. This is primarily because human intelligence is not merely about memory and computing power. It is rooted in consciousness, an input that a machine would never have. Technology's artificial intelligence would place the same interpretation on information every time if the data and the context of that information were the same in each case. Human intelligence will produce results that are not a repetition because each time a conscious input of reasoning would make the outcome a new product. In an intelligence organization every operation is a singular game of human skills even as the same technology upgrades are applied. No technology per se can unravel the enemy's mind unless the side using that technology provides for the human intervention to observe and interpret the data, the signals or the imageries. Being intelligent means being aware that man would achieve better results by using technology but the what and where of the technological aid will always remain in his hands.

Endnotes

1. *Times of India,* Delhi, December 30, 2007.
2. *Doing What Matters,* James M. Kilts, Crown Business NY, 2007

15 Knowledge is Evolutionary

The path of evolution is irreversible. New species come out of the old but stay different. IT revolution is creating new knowledge by setting off innovation and exploration. There is new dialectic and new thinking aiding the evolution of knowledge. What is known cannot become unknown because evolution does not retrace its steps. The age of knowledge has hastened the pace of change and confronted the nations, organizations and individuals with the challenge of change. This challenge is reflected in the transformation that has occurred in the way businesses are transacted today and the new experiences that everyone is exposed to on the personal and work fronts in the information age.

First, there is a general shortening of the life span of anything that is in the nature of a strategic plan. This is because the parameters on which strategy is formulated are affected by new knowledge and the quick change of scene along an unforeseen line. Secondly, issues are cropping up that cannot be resolved through traditional processes like getting additional data on the points earlier examined or breaking the task into smaller problem segments for revalidation. Terrorism, environmental degradation and poverty are problems that have a cause and effect relationship with new knowledge. Unseen causes and unpredictable effects make it difficult to try out a known solution-finding recipe. Terrorism has changed the concept of war as information technology has paved the way for conducting it in 'asymmetric' ways. Lastly, the new surge of man to investigate nature and tame it for the consumers is also causing environmental degradation in newer ways. A connected matter is the reality that poverty is becoming an unwanted offspring of new development anchored on globalization.

It is clear that unprecedented challenges need to be handled with new knowledge and as conventional wisdom alone would not help, new problems have to be put into the matrix of evolving knowledge. Strategy itself has to become an evolving concept and not an absolutist idea. Trial and error will become a legitimate tool for advancement. This in turn will change the concept of 'failure'. A failed mission will not necessarily reflect on the effort and will be reset on the basis of additional inputs of knowledge. Moreover, issues will get intertwined requiring a solution that will come from an integral packaging of knowledge. It is already being felt in the corporate world that the importance of invoking multiplicity of experience at one place had risen rapidly. Solving a problem will involve bending diverse talents together simply because the evolutionary character of knowledge creates situations where nothing is linear or single stranded. Experience or familiarity with the past may not therefore help to address the issue. Instead, an assembly of talents will handle it with greater promise as it will be able to use integrally packaged knowledge more effectively and produce better results in any situation of complexity. Synergy is consequently becoming the new mantra of productivity. It is not difficult to imagine that experience may not necessarily help if the challenge is something that is encountered for the first time-being the product of evolving knowledge.

It can be said that in this age of information many failed strategies would be traceable to 'knowledge fault lines'. In a fast changing world the 'concept of business', the 'statement of purpose' and the 'scope of activities' can all change if new information comes along. If knowledge is evolutionary and therefore unpredictable, strategizing too will have to reckon with such a change. Strategy will have to have a rolling character because it is often based on decisions that have been taken on less then complete information. This is why people who lead change have to be good at 'the management of chaos' and adept at formulating Plan B. They are comfortable with projects that have some open endedness and are inclined to involve innovators and young minds in trying out the marketing mix that suits 'alternate scenarios' and cross culture spreads.

Following the economic melt-down of 2008, the corporate world has realized that in a situation of unpredictable fluctuations that caused tremendous volatility of input costs, it had become extremely critical to plan for and manage the business more dynamically. One way out was to adopt much shorter planning horizons. Hindustan Unilever Limited moved to a continuous 12-monthly planning cycle doing away with the earlier system of annual plans.[1] The rolling plan pattern adopted by HUL confirmed that the economic downturn created the uncertainty of an evolutionary development.

Taking a competent decision on insufficient information, pushing ahead with a somewhat open-ended plan and managing change are the new compulsions created by new knowledge. The borderless markets have thrown up cross-culture operability as a new requirement. This is the time for innovative minds, forward thinkers who can imagine what might happen tomorrow and entrepreneurs who enjoy the excitement of pursuing a mission. The essence of growth triggered by knowledge is that it places premium on the mind not on the muscles. It helps the fittest not the strongest. You will win if you are smart which is a way of saying that you will use intelligence for being in action.

It is primarily because knowledge is evolutionary that we are witnessing an evolution of business too. In what is reminiscent of 'natural selection', today's industries are converging to get the better of the competition. Information technology is throwing open several facets of new knowledge that can be integrated to produce powerful multi-utility products. Nokia's thrust on integrated internet services being made available on mobile phones with emphasis on the local context is creating a new competition among players from different worlds – mobile phones, Apple, Google, Black Burry and Microsoft. Convergence based on compatibility will decide the strength of new businesses in the market. Strategic alliances will be the order of the day in the game of the survival of the fittest. New knowledge will spur the socio-economic evolution in which past practices may not be a good guide and willingness to try out the new turf may hold the key to advancement.

Evolution is the theory that those species survive that are most capable of adapting to the environment as it changes over time. When human beings get together in groups-bringing in their individual preferences, they co-evolve and unity emerges from their diversity because there is a give and take of knowledge amongst them. It is the evolutionary impact of knowledge that creates a situation where the productivity of a group is larger than the sum of the individual productivities. Intelligent organizations encourage such co-evolution of groups within and make sure that an excessive command and control does not thwart this process.

The Indian thought was particularly geared to the concept that knowledge is evolutionary. The reason for this is the fact that Indian thinkers attempted to understand and analyse nature. In exploring the mystery of the universe they came up with some remarkable perceptions of the reality or the absolute, through the path of unfolding knowledge. *Taittiriya Upanishad* records this brilliant observation: 'what is the world? It is the earth below and the sky above and the air in space that connects them. What is light? It is fire below and the sun above and the lightening that connects them. What is education? It is the teacher above and the disciple below and the wisdom that connects them.' This was unraveling knowledge through observation and analysis with imagination thrown in, in adequate measure. Being intelligent means having the willingness to push the envelope in pursuing knowledge on its evolutionary course. The gains will be exclusively yours as you get the new wisdom and benefit from the competitive advantage that it would bring to you.

Learning has to become a habit. If you want to be well informed you have to keep your eyes and ears open so that you can learn from people and the situation around you. You have to ask questions without feeling shy about things that you do not know. Knowledge is unfolding itself all the time. Information has to be updated. Information of the past could easily cease to be a complete resource of knowledge. In professions like medicine and education, experience and contemporariness have to complement each other. Any trainer today has to be a learner also so that he is able to absorb new knowledge evolving in the area of his expertise.

New knowledge impacts both private life as well as the business affairs. In the 1980s the egg industry was in the decline because cholesterol was the mother of all unhealthy food. Then, upon further pursuit, science discovered there was good cholesterol and bad cholesterol and suddenly eggs were allowed back into good graces. In fact, some now call eggs the 'perfect food'.[2]

Just as evolution is classically propelled by entities choosing to come together selectively in a natural way, knowledge evolves when an application of mind and effort is guided by the sense of doing something for the larger good or simply when there is a surge for research to fill in the vacuum created by large gaps in information noticed in a particular sphere or on a particular subject. Evolution of knowledge creates immense possibilities of product variation in business, some surviving better than the others depending upon the perceived utility of their content. Evolving knowledge makes old usages obsolete. Cell phones have caused the fading away of public utility phones operated on coins because, among other things, coins are becoming difficult to acquire. The brutal force of evolution does not permit an earlier product to survive even though there might still be a utility for it.

Knowledge is evolutionary also because it is tracking the path of evolution in nature, all the time. Nothing proves this more effectively than the results of the stem cell research. We are exploring what nature has already kept under the wraps in the stem cells stored in the bone marrow – the blue print of how our organs evolved out of single cells. All innovations are the potential combinations and patterns that nature has already tried out during the journey of evolution, both in the organic and inorganic planes. A new drug, a new instrument and a new cell-function are all uncovered when man reaches a milestone of knowledge trailing the path of evolution. Being intelligent means one should be duly deferential to the connectivity that always exists between what has been and what would be, when rejoicing an achievement or a victory.

The concept of sustainable development is a product of the evolving knowledge that highlights the need for the world of business and industry to become environment friendly. In spite of the discouraging impact of recession on the companies willing to offer eco-friendly products to their customers the fact is that 'sustainability is now the key driver of innovation'[3]. This is quite simply the result of the overpowering influence of knowledge that has in its evolutionary arc, brought environmental concerns to the fore. Just as evolution helped to create new species of life form, advancing knowledge is leading to new next practice platforms such as the smart grid which represents the confluence of digital technology and power saving management of energy drawn from various types of sources. Being intelligent means being aware of the need to be in touch with the new frontiers of knowledge that are potentially altering the socio-economic framework of our times. This is an aspect of being well informed.

Pursuit of a mission is like forging ahead with a headlight. It keeps on making the way for you all the time so long as you are moving. It brings in new knowledge, positive or negative, on the path ahead and also gives you time to opt for a proper response. Any growth, if it is evolutionary, inherently yields things that are new and intelligence lies in being ready to handle knowledge that tosses up a few surprises. An intelligent person uses far-sightedness and tries to decipher what is possibly predictable but he is also prepared to charter an unknown territory while striving for progress.

Endnotes

1. *The Hindu Business Line,* Delhi, June 4, 2009.
2. *Egonomics,* David Marcum & Steven Smith, Simon & Schuster, 2008
3. *Harvard Business Review,* September 2009.

16 Running the Risk

We live in a world that is prone to witnessing unannounced changes in business, politics and environment. Leadership in any sphere of life is tested by the ability of the leader not only to steer through change but in fact lead change to the advantage of those who are following him. The challenge of change implies exposure to the risk of not being able to understand quickly enough the reasons and circumstances that created a new scenario and of being called upon to decide what response would be the most suitable or profitable answer to that situation. Risk essentially involves decision making in an atmosphere of uncertainty and is therefore indirectly proportionate to the completeness of information on which a 'well considered' decision is deemed to have been made.

In the age of knowledge the need to know and know quickly all that can affect your action has become a basic determinant of success. Whether in business or in private life one is in the midst of new information pouring in from all sides. Before you decide to factor in any information for decision making you have to check out for the credibility of the facts or data that the information has brought to you. Intelligent people are trusting but they are never credulous. They are receptive towards information but they always apply their own scan before accepting it. Knowledge of what happened in the past in relation to the matter at hand has its limited utility. The main thing for moving forward on a matter is to have a comprehensive information update on all that was currently happening around that development or context. The fuller is your information reach in the present the better would be the prospect of your being able to foresee what future holds on that front.

Good analysis of information available in the open or that accessed confidentially can produce intelligence which by definition is knowledge that gives you a peep into the future. Intelligence naturally is what makes you a winner in any process of knowledge based decision making. Businesses, not surprisingly, are making a lot of investment on securing competitive intelligence. Getting to know of what the competition was up to or how the competitive environ would shape up in the period ahead, mitigates the risk that would be there for your own plan of action. Today skills of intelligence gathering are employed by the corporates who may sometimes be even crossing the legal and ethical boundaries in the process. The fact however remains that just as intelligence is an important weapon with which a nation safeguards its security, today's enterprises facing global competition need competitive intelligence both to protect themselves as well as to steal a march over the rivals.

Information of intelligence value is always difficult to secure directly. A lot of it can be distilled out of information that is available in the public domain, through competent analysis. However, the challenge of decision making often is that action has to be launched on information that is incomplete in the sense of not being able to define the exact moves of the adversary even though the nature of the game was indicated. In another setting it may identify the market forces but not be clear about the consequences they will produce. You can therefore proceed with your plan in the right direction but be prepared to take on the uncertainties that come up on the way. Risk is inherent in a situation where ambiguity exists but in a sense it is part of life because complete clarity is difficult to come by in any situation. However, remember that it is good to take risks but not good to be ignorant of them. Just as ignorance of law is no excuse, being oblivious of the hazards of the competitive environ of which you are a part, cannot protect you from a possible exposure to harm. The analysts of the National Security Agency in the US have adopted the methodology of reflecting intelligence that was less than complete, by reporting that the concerned National Intelligence Estimate (NIE) was based on 'moderate to high' confidence.

Before you launch a business or any other operation on a territory you have to be well informed on the state of the market there, the technological advancement of the country, its legal and political system, the law and order situation and even the socio-cultural disposition of the people. Knowledge of the elements that determine the competitive environ around you will tend to minimize the risk that your enterprise might otherwise encounter. A smart corporation understands the importance of intelligence in the formulation of business plans and has its members equipped with the ability to harness and use information of intelligence value for the betterment of the enterprise. Today we need information savvy leaders to direct business activity.

Forward thinking and a conscious effort to imagine what lies beyond the picture established by the analysis of the available information, controls the risk matrix that exists around any new entrepreneurship. The concept of 'lateral thinking' is particularly relevant here.[1] It contends that the human mind is gifted with the ability not only to logically analyze the information that was available but also to anticipate what the others might be thinking in a given situation. Lateral thinking reinforces imagination which in turn helps to project knowledges on to the unseen path that lay ahead. It facilitates the perception of what your rivals might do on that turf. This in fact is what intelligence is all about. Being intelligent means being smart about risk taking.

How much risk could an organization settle for is something that is a part of the leadership function. Risk is taken at the level where the buck stops so far as the accountability is concerned. Risk connects with decision making in a situation where there is choice of alternative actions. The right course of action would be dictated by your being sure about what the analysis of the available information reveals and your insight into the likely consequences of your moves. Taking risk is, therefore, not the same thing as gambling because in the case of gambling there is no means of knowing at all how the process will play out. Intelligent people take a risk with full awareness of the intangibles that surround their decision making. The dynamics of unpredictability may still exist around a considered decision because of the gaps that were there in the information base. Colin Powell, the then US Secretary of State is reported to have told his Intelligence analysts: 'tell me what you know, then tell me what you don't know and always keep those separated'.[2] This is the approach that would help the leader to remain prepared for dealing with the risk that was implicit in his action.

It stands to reason that strong delivery that works around a team that is determined 'to beat the deadlines', a keen lookout for anything that would add value to the project at hand and maintaining a capability of doing a mid-course correction in response to a new insight into the competitive environ, represent a mix of competencies that might convert risk into an opportunity. Risk is on the whole getting connected with the questions like how well-informed the decision taker is, how enthusiastic is the implementation and how intrepid is the organization about carrying a difficult game through. Interestingly globalization can both mitigate and enhance risk as the impact of economic downturn of 2008 has amply shown. Countries, companies and consumers who were thinking 'globally' are feeling compelled to think 'locally' again to rebuild their lives and businesses. Globalization continues to have relevance but as the centricity of the developed West in driving the world's economic trends weakened, the local needs, local consumer base and the local sociology have acquired added importance. You cannot borrow from other models beyond a point as you have to work out of your own systems, your own strengths and your own intelligence. You have to run your risks within your own situation. Being intelligent means being on the local- global grid that best works for you. Globalization compels the movement towards modernization and modernization has to reckon with the fact that it is the socio-cultural profile of the people that determines the attitude to work, perception of a thing like the leisure time, consumer's preferences, boss-subordinate relationship and even the work-life balance.

Risk mitigation demands that errors of omission must be eliminated. These come in the way of the company getting the best dividends out of the investment of time made by it. Also, failure of some action today may deny you the long term benefits. If there is no action there is no risk. As TS Eliot said: 'only those who risk going too far can possibly find out how far they can go'. The farther ahead you can see, the less risk your actions will generate. Absence of far-sightedness in action is also therefore an omission that can influence the outcome. Intelligence backed initiatives get you the best results and save you from many avoidable risks. They make an organization pro-active, optimistic and intrepid.

At the core of all business is the financial risk that an enterprise and its management take for their initiatives. The economic melt-down of 2008 has made out the case for an effective oversight at the national and international levels on the goings-on in the markets, the fair play in competition, role of the Board of Directors, regulation of banking, compensation package for the corporate leaders and the ethical running of the corporate bodies in general. Management of physical risk and loss prevention had predictably emerged as the top concerns for all enterprises. Security is based on the fundamental thought that virtually all loss is preventable. Reliance Retail took an early lead in demonstrating that loss prevention engineering could be made an effective instrument of control in this area of security. In the hard segment of security, 9/11 reduced the relevance of mathematical modelling for mitigating risk and pushed to the fore the 'case scenario' approach that rested on real time threat assessments. Being intelligent means making it your business to know all about the security environ of the country in which you live or operate. Remember, threats to the security of any establishment is both external and internal, the damage in a major proportion of cases being caused by a disloyal or subversive insider.

The most visible risk to any business thus comes from the security concerns that prevail in the area or the country where your enterprise is located. The threats of terrorism, insurgency and proxy wars have sharply increased in the post-cold war period. The threat to physical security is followed by the risks arising out of the degree of political stability and government effectiveness. In the Indian context, as would be the case with many other countries of the developing world, corruption is a major problem at all levels of authority with politicians and officials routinely demanding bribes in return for awarding contracts or tenders.[3] No business house should ever treat this as an opportunity for gaining competitive advantage. Further, the regulatory system may not be immune from policy reversals due to pressure from vested interests and inter-ministry rivalries. The state of development of infrastructure is another factor relevant to the evaluation of risk. Labour relations that determine the prospects of strike action become an important factor in risk analysis too, particularly for the private sector.

Risk is reduced if there is quality assurance in all the segments of the enterprise. Delivery time schedules often generate pressures that undermine this function, silently subverting the processes, credibility and ultimately the profitability of the company. The security architecture, for instance, will need to be checked upon randomly through mock drills, short term audits and walkthroughs or spot inspections. The supervision protocols should all be focused on uncovering and remedying any defect that is encountered, whether it is in the organizational structure, operational process, communication system, performance appraisal or trial runs. Correcting a fault is a contingency that should elicit the same level of response as is kept reserved for an external threat. Quick action on a contingency of any kind is a definite mitigation of risk. Being intelligent means being cognizant of the internal weaknesses in your establishment as much as being focused on the dangers from outside to which you think you are vulnerable. Internal vigilance and intelligence on the external threats are the facets of the integral security of any entity.

The risk for an enterprise comes from the probability of a natural disaster, the identified sources of threat to the security of the country or the territory where the establishment is located, the threats that are specific to the organization because of the nature of its operations and output, placing of the company in the competitive market and the sheer vulnerability of its processes to a subverted insider. There has to be an analysis for each of these categories so that counter-measures can be made more relevant, lasting and cost-effective. The solutions should aim at prevention but should ensure that there is prompt remedial handling in the event of a breach or loss taking place. The risk horizon, like any security scenario, is not static and, therefore, evaluation of risk has to be done periodically. It also has to allow for assimilation of a new risk cropping up suddenly and a quick revision of response to deal with the change. The assessment of risk has to be both long term as well as in the short time frame to work out integral solutions. The effort should be to minimize the area of uncertainty in risk analysis. This will happen if the organization and its leaders are information savvy and have the wherewithal to garner intelligence about the potential risks. In ultimate analysis risk evaluation is all about forecasting the future and doing this correctly. Moreover, analysis and decision making cannot hang fire indefinitely for complete intelligence to come by. This is why handling risk calls for a dynamic leadership that can see an opportunity ahead of others even when the road is a little hazy and then go for it in the spirit of adventure and not gambling.

Running the risk is relatable to the degree of effort made to make business investments only after taking a considered view of the prospects that they would offer, formulate an effective loss prevention plan and draw up a security strategy for the establishment on the basis of a proper vulnerability assessment. Expenditure incurred on anything that provides physical security and prevents loss were now considered an integral part of the basic financial outlay for a project or an organization. This is a new thinking that the new age we live in has brought with it.

It is not possible to make a decision that is totally free of risk because, as mentioned earlier, one cannot have a complete idea of what lies ahead even if one had the best available business intelligence at hand. Three things need to be kept in mind while taking a decision. First, it is good to concede that the process of decision-making is helped by the experience you have had of what has gone by in that sphere of activity. However, any decision prima facie is basically about what is to happen now or what will be done from now on. This means that you have to be prepared for something that did not necessarily occur in the past and would not therefore be covered in the ambit of 'experience'. Good risk takers are open to new readings about what could happen in the future. Secondly, an awareness of the macro picture of which your activity or enterprise is a part, is very important. This helps avert the danger of your taking a uni-focal examination of risk and running into a problem when some facet of the competitive environment that had missed your attention, came up as a roadblock. Finally, risk management will always be strengthened by the flexibility that you bring to bear upon your plan of execution or delivery to make alterations without causing too many jolts. The scenario of partial certainty that is now with us all the time in the new age of information, calls for a switch over to 'rolling plans' that admit of mid-course corrections necessitated by an unforeseen development. Being intelligent means taking a risk with awareness so that you would not be surprised to the point of feeling unsettled should the course of events not turn out to be what was anticipated.

Endnotes

1. *The Biography of Edward de Bono* by Piers Dudgeon, Headline Book Publishing, London 2001
2. *The Inheritance* by David E. Sanger, Bantam Press London 2009
3. *Business India Intelligence,* Oct 21, 2009

17 The Age of Intelligence

If the information technology revolution opened the doors to the 'age of knowledge', the globalization of human thought and endeavour is compelling another paradigm shift towards what can be described as the 'age of intelligence'. It is intelligence and not mere information that would bring in success in a scenario where information is shared universally no sooner than it is produced. Being intelligent would mean being in a position to cull out of this information an insight into what lies ahead, through analysis, imagination or innovation. Success will come more easily to those who have a mind-set that is needed to appreciate the global applicability or dimension of any development, product or process.

Globalization is adding value to the feasibility of an individual or an organisation being able to locate several functions or operations across the globe and integrate them into one corporate entity. In other words intelligent global players are getting more and more integrally packaged. The pharmaceutical company, Smith Cline Beecham became a global giant as a result of the integration of Smith Cline – strong in marketing and Beecham whose main strength was in R&D. Knowledge becomes most rewarding when its integral packaging is complete. Fruitful mergers, takeovers and acquisitions are based on due diligence which is an intelligence exercise. Being intelligent will be the defining hallmark of successful corporates and professionals in the age of intelligence.

The socio-economic development of the future is likely to promote a trend in which politics of economy will supersede the politics of community. In the age of intelligence language and regional barriers are bound to get de-emphasized because intelligent people will see through the counter productive dimension of the conflicts caused by cultural or geographical fault-lines. Considering that in the post-cold war era the graph of violent movements aimed at asserting cultural identity by way of insurgencies, cross-border terrorism and proxy wars, has registered an upward move, this stipulation is yet to be tested. However, it is expected that the leaders in public life and the drivers of economic globalization would see to it that intelligence prevails over emotions in guiding their decisions. Intelligent nations, communities, organizations and individuals are bound to opt for mutual cooperation for the larger good against the misdemeanors of the deviant fundamentalist and the destructive few. The natural enlargement of benevolent cross-border transactions and people to people interactions will make this a feature of the emerging age of intelligence.

Intelligence will be a useful tool for unraveling the opportunities that bring benefit to all shareholders and not merely for the narrow purpose of cutting down a rival. Globalization will eventually lay the ground-work for intelligence sharing amongst the forces of the 'good' to counter the scattered malcontents. Shared prosperity will soften the impact of the minority of political leaders engaged in serving their vested interest by whipping up agitation in the name of voicing discontent of their groups or communities. In the age of intelligence economic disparities and not political rights will be the root cause of conflicts.

For this welcome shift to occur in favour of economic progress over political attainment, the capitalist growth resting entirely on liberalization, free enterprise and profit will have to be tempered with a sense of obligation for addressing human security concerns. The corporate social responsibility is going to be an important benchmark for any business aspiring to succeed globally. The 'corporate' citizen will be called upon to establish credibility of its strategy in this sphere to get the support of the State. Socially responsible economic growth will be the pattern of development in future. This will happen not because of any pull of ideology but solely out of necessity for global stability needed by international business.

In border-less markets there is a new logic and a new compulsion shaping up the old capitalist economy. The economic melt-down of 2008 in the USA leading the government there to release a bail out package of 700 billion dollars drew attention to the need for a systemic oversight to avert financial mismanagement in the corporate world and minimize the chances of individual's greed supplanting business ethics. To seek an unbroken rise in profits the firms will have to join in the efforts to expand the market. There cannot be an expansion of the market in a global sense unless the number of people with purchasing power increases effectively. In India, for instance, 20-25% of the population commands the total purchasing power, which pretty much corresponds to the situation existing globally outside of the developed world. Inequality feeds the classical capitalist system as the human engines of production work for the owners of the businesses and the owners of wealth seek recourse to armament to subdue any challenge to production. The failure of international Communism shown by the demise of the USSR demonstrated the pitfalls of a system where the State totally controlled economy like a dictator would control polity. In the new post-cold war years the alternate capitalist economic system driven totally by free market and profit has begun to prove ineffective. What is worse, it has tended to give legitimacy to the economically and politically disgruntled forces resorting to the new weapon of terrorism to set off an 'asymmetric' warfare against the stronger enemy.

The economic melt-down highlighted the importance of being cost-effective in running business operations and this, in turn, called for a greater need for the management to have detailed, updated and unadulterated information about what was happening. A good contingency response, business analysts rightly underlined, depended on a correct evaluation of how bad the situation for an enterprise was and how bad it could get. Those who got this right did a better job of dealing with the crisis. Du Pont is reported to have asked its employees to identify three things they could do immediately to help conserve cash and reduce costs.[1] Travel was curtailed sharply, internal meetings were cancelled, consultants and contractors were eliminated where possible, the team dealing with issues of security and plant safety was asked to stand down and employees were taken into confidence about the roots of the slow-down. The melt-down tested the leadership of business heads, particularly their decision-making, far-sightedness and nerves. The crisis also revealed that weak internal controls, brazen disregard for lending standards and accounting jugglery substantially contributed to the fall of many business giants.

Information technology has given boost to the economic globalization but it has also helped the terrorists in the planning of covert attacks. Intelligent leaders of economy and business therefore realize that not only will the workers and producers have to be kept satisfied about their compensations but the profit makers will also have to, additionally, contribute to the human resource development in the society so that more and more people could join in the economic mainstream reducing the turf that militants were able to exploit. In the Indian context the widely spread Maoist movement with trans-national links is a case study to test the doctrine that free enterprise combined with equitable growth can possibly alleviate economic disparities that do lie at the root of this insurgency, at least partially. In the age of intelligence economic development will seek to reduce these disparities. Economic classes will exist but there will be opportunity for advancement for all so that frustration driven recourse to militancy will be less in evidence.

Technology is producing newer products and services. In the age of intelligence their turnover will be faster because of innovations. With passage of time, however, the equation between the desire and the need will tend to become more balanced because of which some intermediate technologies will come to stay in terms of the comfort level sought by the users. Some classes will always be there, pursuing the state of the art lifestyles at any cost. Technology will produce more jobs and help to reduce poverty by putting skill development above the conventional 'paper' degrees of education. For a nation like India the smart strategy is to emphasize skill development training through a network of modern and resourceful polytechnics at the grass root level where the boys and girls completing school or college education can get admission without hassle and undergo a training of their choice. The biggest challenge for India is to upgrade the human infrastructure. Subsidized residential Polytechnics are a major instrument for dealing with this formidable task. We need to produce thousands of professional hands for plumbing, electric repairs, computer assistance, masonry and paramedical work.

A National Sample Survey Organisation study indicated that 58% of the employable population of India was unemployed in 2004-05. The Government of India Economic Survey 2006-07 acknowledged a rise in unemployment and decline in employment in the organized sector and termed it 'worrisome'. With the Indian demographic shifts over the next 10-15 years bringing in millions more into the age groups of 10-20 and 20-30, unemployment is expected to become an even bigger problem particularly in the rural sector. In such a scenario it was not difficult to imagine that the Maoist movement might register an expansion putting a further strain on the law and order machinery in the soft belly of India. The economic recession of 2008 sparked off by the US makes it even more important for India to follow a balanced strategy that combines globalization with a far more intense growth of home industry and infrastructure. Creation of skilled hands of high standards should primarily serve the indigenous needs.

In the age of intelligence that is now upon us, there will be attitudinal changes and shifts in the outlook of the society on many matters. Decision-making will be more an exercise of mind and not a by-product of muscle power. Failures on the work front will be considered redeemable and not catastrophic because lack of success will be looked upon as an effort that did not hit the bull's eye even though it did get somewhere. Being intelligent would mean being there when the order of nature brings you another opportunity. Trying out another option will be the new philosophy of life and no situation will be regarded as the end of the road. Learning from experience and looking for an innovative change of track will come more naturally to people who are in pursuit of an objective. New manufacture, services, applications, end users and ways of sharing time will create work for many more hands. The global networks on all fronts will multiply generating local employment for multinational players in business, NGOs and social sectors like health and education. Optimism, application and willingness to try out something new will characterize entrepreneurship.

The globalization of economy has predictably unraveled the need for a global social policy even as the political world order remains pretty well identified with the sovereign nations trying to benefit from the rise of border-less markets and developing stakes in promoting international peace. Pulls and pressures between the North and the South, between the developed world and the developing nations, and between the global players and the regional groupings are no doubt arising at forums like the WTO but the good news is that civil society organisations are emerging as a new force that would work for establishing level playing fields and building a consensus for priority being accorded to the global mission of providing human security to people everywhere. Launched from regional settings, civil society organizations are becoming the key protagonists of integration of people among the neighbouring countries. They will have to complement the global missions and not become a source of resistance to the one world movement in the name of promoting regional alternatives. When the political divides are becoming notional, socio-cultural convergence among the people needs to be built up to bring in the best advantage of economic globalization to all parts of the world. The age of intelligence will facilitate this transition.

The age of intelligence will keep up the challenge of change. Ever since the IT revolution steered the make over from the industrial age to the age of knowledge, handling change has become the biggest imperative for all leaders, entrepreneurs and professionals. To be able to lead change is the single most important requisite for success. A new mind-set is needed to accept the reality that change is the norm now. Being intelligent means understanding the inevitability of change and making even change an orderly process. If you are attitudinally well prepared for change and know about what and why of it, you would develop a certain fearlessness about the unknown and be able to deal with it with confidence.

In the age of intelligence rapid changes in the competition and the competitive environ will call for a dynamic approach to strategizing that allows for enrichment of the content in the light of new knowledge and adoption of tactical alterations to respond to the shifts in the external scene. Being attuned to the nuances of what is happening around us, never underestimating the competitors and pushing ahead on your own strengths to chase an opportunity, is a mix that would sustain intelligent people and organisations.

The age of intelligence will create a new yardstick for grading the employees of a business or professional outfit on the basis of their capacity to make use of knowledge to add value to whatever they were doing. For those handling the human resource development, the new task would be to convert the work force, earlier looked upon as a manual congregation, to an assembly of knowledge workers each of whom is an individual source of productivity. The emphasis will shift from training him for a prescribed function to getting him to a responsibility where his talent finds its best expression. The assembly lines will have smart sequencing to make for a failsafe production and this will be made possible by technology enabled monitoring carried out by an intelligent work force.

It is not too difficult to imagine that economic globalization will have to pass through three distinct phases of development, which reflect the play of intelligence during this transition. We already see this happening. In the first, the forces behind the borderless markets will have to contend with and even confront issues of political sovereignty invoked by national governments whose concern naturally would be to ensure that home industries got a level playing field against the foreign companies. In 1993, Warren Christopher, Secretary of State in the Clinton administration enunciated that 'national security is inseparable from economic security' to lay down a strategy that would help corporate America to deal with the 'unfair' treatment meted out to the US enterprises in some countries. A part of this strategy was to share information of intelligence value compiled by the US intelligence agencies on the competitive environ in different parts of the world, with the US companies. A natural leveler that would become prominent in this phase, would rise from the situation that the new competition would tend to provide opportunities of growth to smaller but more efficient players. Ultimately the temptation to play politics with economy will get watered down as globalization makes steady progress.

In the second phase, the multinational conglomerates will become crucial drivers of globalization exercising a significant influence on international relations. Regional groupings may emerge in the process to facilitate the moves of the corporates to integrate their operational and infrastructural activities across the national frontiers and cultural divides. A pharmaceutical company may integrate with its research labs situated thousands of miles away and banks may dish out various products suiting the people in different socio-economic environment. Managers who can work in multicultural settings will also be in great demand and they will collectively tend to unite the world in their own way.

It is the third sequential phase of economic globalization, which will decide if the age of intelligence moves in the direction of ensuring 'the largest good of the largest people' or creates a new form of economic imperialism and global conflicts. State controlled economies are beginning to fall aside for good, which is a positive sign. However, the capitalist model of economic growth relying totally on free market and profit that made a few richer at the cost of all others will come in under the pressure of correction. The melt-down of 2008 beginning from the US set off this trend. The age of intelligence will, by helping to expand the market all the time and bringing in newer customers and consumers, mitigate any exploitative shifts in the conduct of businesses. Much will depend on whether competitive intelligence is used by businesses to corner short-term advantages or is utilized in the pursuit of opportunities that bring in gains in the long range. One should hope that the idea of socially responsible economic growth will prevail over lesser objectives simply because there would be no other option worth its while, available. It would do a lot of good to all nations if human development and removal of stark disparities are consciously pursued as the objective of the millennium. Information age has helped to empower people as it is enabling everybody to be informed of the truth of their economic, political and cultural circumstances. The crafted pronouncements of the governments will not hold and the less privileged will not remain quite and isolated[2].

Disparities will become the focus in a people-centric world. Economic inequalities will lead to conflicts and if they coincide with 'cultural fault lines' they could produce a war as destructive as any world war could possibly be. The post-cold war years have already demonstrated the gravity of this kind of drift towards a new asymmetric warfare that uses terrorism as a weapon. The national and corporate leaders need to be intelligent about their policies and strategies if they want to make the world a better place.

Endnotes

1. *Business Week*, McGraw Hill, Jan 19, 2009.
2. *What Will Be*, Michael Dertouzos, Harper Edge, 1997.

Index